INDIGENOUS ACTIVISM IN THE MIDWEST

INDIGENOUS ACTIVISM IN THE MIDWEST

Refusal, Resurgence, and Resisting Settler Colonialism

Margret McCue-Enser

MICHIGAN STATE UNIVERSITY PRESS | *East Lansing*

Michigan State University Press
East Lansing, Michigan 48823-5245

Library of Congress Cataloging-in-Publication Data
Names: McCue-Enser, Margret author
Title: Indigenous activism in the Midwest : refusal, resurgence, and resisting settler colonialism / Margret McCue-Enser.
Description: East Lansing : Michigan State University Press, 2025. | Includes bibliographical references and index.
Identifiers: LCCN 2025005370 | ISBN 9781611865509 paperback | ISBN 9781609177935 | ISBN 9781628955569
Subjects: LCSH: Indians of North America—Minnesota—Historiography | Settler colonialism—Minnesota | Memorialization—Social aspects—Minnesota | Public spaces—Social aspects—Minnesota | Historic sites—Social aspects—Minnesota
Classification: LCC E78.M7 .M33 2025 | DDC 977.6/00497—dc23/eng/20250404
LC record available at https://lccn.loc.gov/2025005370

Rhetoric of Power and Protest
Series Editors: Leroy Dorsey and Shawn Parry-Giles

Book design by Anastasia Wraight
Cover art is an image of a prairie pothole under a dramatic
pink sky at sunset with sky reflection in pond, Adobe Stock / Midwest Imagery

---

Visit Michigan State University Press at *www.msupress.org*

Contents

Preface

This is the jingle dress dance right here. This right here is a healing dance. See, what they're doing here is the circle, see the circle? This is the circle of life. What these dancers are doing is they're crying not only for themselves, for the safety of their families, but also for you guys. And also a healing for everybody. We can't do this without the drums. Each step is a prayer. So we can't do our prayers without the drums.

—Speaker at George Floyd Square, "Jingle Dress Healing Dance for George Floyd at the Corner of 38th and Chicago Where He Was Murdered in Minneapolis," Women's Indigenous Media Facebook

In the days following the 2020 murder of George Floyd by a Minneapolis police officer, the intersection of Chicago and 38th was transformed from a site of violence and death to one of prayer and persistence. A jingle dance that was held at the site reconstituted the place from one of police violence to one of Indigenous and Black resilience. In a video posted on Women's Indigenous Media's Facebook page, a speaker explained that the jingle dance is a ceremony, a collective prayer.[1] Native American Studies professor and member of the Red Lake Ojibwe tribe, Brenda Child, writes about the jingle dress dance in her book *Holding Our World Together: Ojibwe Women and the Survival of Community*. A ceremony that survived despite being banned for much of the twentieth century, Child explains that the jingle dance is made up of "both songs and dresses [that] contain a strong therapeutic value." Child continues, the women dance "to ensure the health and well-being of an individual, their family, or even the broader tribal community."[2] The jingle dress dancers brought healing and attention to the Black and Indigenous communities of Minnesota who continue to face discrimination and harassment.[3] Just as the jingle dress dance survived despite its being banned, Indigenous connection to place reflects existence and resistance.

Using specific places as a way of expressing unity and resilience at crucial times is an important part of Indigenous activism. In an interview with Canadian Broadcasting Corporation Indigenous News, local activist Lisa Skjefte, who helped coordinate the drummers for the George Floyd jingle dress dance, explained that Indigenous and Black residents unite in the fight against racism. Skjefte states, "[t]his kind of unity that's bringing people together, it's the kind of thing that's going to help us battle systems of oppression."[4] A crucial part of the "battle against systems of oppression" is uniting and reclaiming these places, such as George Floyd square, in which systems of oppression are most visible and thereby contestable. The activists' assertion of Indigenous and BIPOC (Black, Indigenous, and people of color) agency at the place in which it was most violently cut down works to make this violence visible as well as to assert BIPOC resilience. Jingle dances and other forms of ceremony assert Indigenous being and connection to place, as such they are a form of activism.

Jingle dances have been used by Indigenous activists to assert Indigenous connection to place and interrupt, expose, and complicate non-Indigenous claims to place. Globally recognized groups such as Idle No More use ritual and dance to assert Indigenous rights to place. Idle No More is an inter-tribal group formed in 2012 whose work intersects with opposition to Line Three in Minnesota. On December 29, 2013, the group held a Round Dance flash mob at the Mall of America (MOA), prompting threats of arrest if future dances were held.[5] In her essay "Aambe! Maajaadaa! (What #IdleNoMore Means to Me)," founder and Indigenous studies scholar Leanne Betasamosake Simpson explains, "I stand up anytime our nation's land base is threatened because everything we have of meaning comes from the land—our political systems, our intellectual systems, our health care, food security, language and our spiritual sustenance and our moral fortitude."[6] The jingle dance is a way of making visible and accessible Indigenous connection to place, particularly at those places and times in which that connection is "threatened." At both at the MOA rotunda and George Floyd square, ceremony reflected and reinforced Indigenous and BIPOC being and belonging.

In choosing such public places at such poignant times, the activists at George Floyd Square and the MOA assert Indigenous systems and ways of being and in doing so seize and shift attention from settler colonialism. Settler colonialism is a concept that refers not to settlement as an event, but to the legal, economic, and socio-cultural systems that engineer and perpetuate the elimination of Indigenous people and lifeways.[7] Holding a jingle dance at George Floyd Square asserts not just Indigenous resilience and healing but also exposes and interrogates police violence toward Black and Indigenous people.[8] Holding a jingle dance at MOA asserts Indigenous being and exposes the relationship between consumerism and the extraction of natural resources. That these events take place at a particular site and in conjunction with a particular event is what lends them particular poignancy. This book focuses on how Indigenous activists assert being and belonging at specific places and times and the ways in which this rhetoric reflects and reasserts Indigenous agency and exposes settler colonialism. As a contemporary rhetorical studies scholar interested in public arguments about land and belonging in Minnesota, I focus on Indigenous activism and settler colonialism.

In this book, I examine sites of public memory and the ways in which Indigenous relations to these places are made visible via the material and discursive and visual rhetoric at and about these places. I analyze built spaces and discourses to identify the ways in which activists assert Indigenous logics of place and time and, thereby, expose and intervene in settler colonialist logics.[9] First, I show how Indigenous relationships to place is sacred and how this relationship is central to Indigenous activism. Second, I demonstrate how Indigenous activists assert Indigenous epistemologies of place and time and in doing so challenge and rework the terms of recognition. Third, I explain how Indigenous activism makes visible and accessible ways to reimagine place and one's relationship with it outside of settler colonialist systems.

These case studies elucidate the nuances of how Indigenous refusal, as Indigenous studies scholar Betasamosake Simpson explains, works to assert Indigeneity. Refusal is generative of Indigenous recognition. Put another way, Indigenous recognition is made possible via refusal of state logics of recognition. Indigenous land relations, though, are tied up literally and logistically in state and federal land management. These case studies reveal how Indigenous land relations are negotiated and articulated outside of and despite state recognition. "Radical resurgence," according to Betasamosake Simpson, is refusal of "state recognition as an organizing platform and mechanism for dismantling systems of colonial domination" and "state's framing of issues" and instead to "re-embed these issues within Indigenous political contexts and realities."[10] I rely heavily on Indigenous scholarship to do this analysis.

I use Indigenous epistemologies and methods so as to not just analyze Indigenous rhetoric on its own terms, but also as part of the larger effort to decolonize my own field of communication studies. Critical Indigenous studies, also referred to as Native American studies, as Aileen Moreton-Robinson explains, is "a knowledge/power domain in whereby scholars operationalize Indigenous knowledges to develop theories, build academic infrastructure, and inform our cultural and ethical practices."[11] I gather the work of Indigenous scholars who articulate the centrality of "grounded normativity" or the idea that one's relationship with place is the center of the universe for that person and community. I put Indigenous activism here in Minnesota in direct conversation with settler colonialism. I do this because land is the central tenant of both, and following this, I believe that focusing on competing conceptualizations of land helps us to understand the relationship between land ownership, agrarianism, and nation building.

As I focus on places of historical importance, I draw on the field of memory studies, which is the exploration of how communities curate, preserve, and promote places as narratives of the past which, thereby, provide guidance for the present and future.[12] As a contemporary rhetorical studies scholar interested in examining historical place and discourses about them, I employ spatial and discursive analysis. I rely on Samantha Senda-Cook, Michael K. Middleton, and Danielle Endres who explain the work of in situ analysis as "a socially constructed place imbued with meaning(s) that simultaneously enables, constrains, and constitutes rhetorical practices."[13] In conducting spatial analysis of sites, I examine how the material environment enabled movement and access to some places and meanings and foreclosed access to other places and meanings. The material environment of the places that are included in these case studies includes walkways, signage, buildings, building footings or remnants, and other material objects like rocks, trees, waterways, prairies, gardens, as well as other visitors and staff. I use discursive and visual analysis to identify the reoccurring and therefore key themes across person-to-person spoken communication, websites whether in written and/or audio-visual text, newspaper stories in written text and photographic images, and finally, books, dissertations, and articles. This project makes a number of important contributions to Indigenous studies, settler colonialism studies, and communication studies.

First, these case studies build on the work of critical Indigenous studies scholars like Glen Coulthard, Audra Simpson, Betasamosake Simpson, and others and explicate the nuances of recognition and refusal as a strategy through which Indigenous communities articulate their relationships with specific places. I believe my work is in conversation with Audra Simpson and her analysis of the Kahnawà:ke because, while she uses ethnographic methods to identify and examine how individuals and communities navigate refusal as generative of Indigeneity, I employ material and discursive analysis to examine how larger communities and movements negotiate resistance and refusal. Both studies examine how Indigenous communities turn inward so as to constitute Indigenous lifeways as resistance and subsistence. While Simpson explores activism on the micro level and mine on the macro, our common interest lies in what she terms these "geopolitical spaces," or making visible how Indigenous activism is most importantly an act of Indigenous sovereignty and not simply a response to settler colonialism.[14] In fact, I argue that the case studies I explore make visible how articulations of settler colonialism specifically as it is generated from or tied to specific places provides perhaps unique opportunities for Indigenous sovereignty to assert itself and for the structures and sutures of settler colonialism to be revealed and unraveled.

Second, by centering Indigenous epistemologies of place as not only as the object, but especially the method of analysis, this analysis reveals the ways in which settler colonialism is inscribed within contemporary rhetorical conceptualizations of place and memory studies. Specifically, this project extends the work of Ryan Casey Kelly and Jason Black to decolonize rhetorical and related fields of study not only by exploring how local Indigenous communities assert existence but by grounding analysis in Indigenous epistemologies. Settler colonialism informs dominant conceptualizations of place as an object or commodity to be claimed, named, and exchanged. The premise of memory studies, that the past exists as something apart from the present and future, is also imbued with settler colonialism. This study aims to cultivate the larger conversation within contemporary rhetorical studies and related fields about how, left unexamined, the guiding assumptions of our fields contribute to the marginalization of Indigeneity.[15]

This analysis intersects with the rich body of Indigenous scholarship that brings theory as it is lived and created by communities into the academy. Communication studies scholar Tiara Na'puti argues a "coarticulated frame" of Indigenous Studies and rhetorical studies "reveals contradictions, limitations, and complexities to hold rhetorical studies accountable—for its enduring dearth of engagement with indigeneity."[16] This discussion centers Indigenous studies and Indigeneity as both method and object of study. In this way, this work aligns with and builds on that of Romeo García and Damían Baca who, as they explain, "practice epistemic disobedience."[17] García and Baca focus on what they explain as the "local, everyday 'vernacular' knowledges" as a way to map where and how lived experience gives way to and marks paths of decolonial resistance. I employ spatial and discursive analysis to demarcate where and how Indigenous existence negotiates terms of refusal and recognition. Indeed, this book not only answers Na'puti and others' call for Indigenous scholarship within communication studies and related fields, but it centers it as a body of theory and method.

Third, by leaning into Indigenous and settler colonialist logics we are able to see the points of clash between the two and, more specifically, the ways in which settler place logics are inherently self-circumscribing. By centering Indigenous conceptualizations of place, we are able to see how a place has significance outside of settler logics of ownership as well as how simply the articulation of Indigenous land relations pulls at these now exposed seams. This collection builds on scholarship by Michael Lechuga, García and Baca, and others who work at the intersection of contemporary rhetorical and Indigenous studies. These case studies make visible and accessible not only the role that place plays as the spiritual and cultural center of Indigenous communities, but more specifically, in terms of contemporary rhetorical studies and beyond, that a failure to account for this in our respective ontologies will undermine our epistemologies.

Fourth, analyzing Indigenous land logics alongside agrarian land logics deepens understanding not just of settler colonialism, but specifically agrarianism as it is tied the frontier myth and nation building. In an era that has seen a resurgence in nativist discourses such as replacement theory and the like, it is important to explicate how land memory works to fasten specific terms of belonging.[18] The hegemonic force of white settler agrarianism shapes not only a Midwestern regional imaginary, but also the national ethos. From its founding to the present day, Minnesota continues both economically and culturally to be an agrarian state. These competing ideologies of place and time bear the need for much closer examination. This project intersects with Lechuga's examination of the role that science fiction film plays in constructing and circulating the invading alien as a trope against which settler citizen subjectivities and control over land are legitimized.[19] While Lechuga examines science fiction, and this analysis explores place and representations of it, our shared interest is exploring how the Indigenous/Other/BIPOC figure is constructed and circulated as a way of legitimating the settler citizen subject as part of the maintenance of settler colonialist systems.

It is not simply that method emerges from place, but that accessing Indigenous relations with said place is the only way to fully understand and engage with it. Lechuga argues that Indigenous studies is the way to "denaturaliz[e] practices of settler reproduction and [to] recognize practices of knowledge production that happen outside of the halls of the academy." Critically reflecting on his work with a political activist group, No Papers, No Fear Movement, Lechuga argues that the field of rhetorical studies largely reflects settler colonialism in the ways that knowledge creation and dissemination follows extractivist principles. Instead, Lechuga advances the argument that activism be considered "not as an object of study but, rather, a source of knowledge akin to theory."[20] From this, it follows that research becomes a relationship with communities doing activist work. Indigenous activism reflects place relations. To fully understand and engage with Indigenous logics therefore requires understanding Indigenous place relations and how it informs activism.

This preface is organized around the three objectives for the book. In the first section, "Contestations of Memory and Place," I begin with a brief recap of the fields of memory studies and rhetorical analysis of place as well as how they inform this project. Next, I explain the Indigenous concept of grounded normativity and how it accounts for not just the relationship one has with place, but how that relationship is the basis and guidance for everything. I draw on research from Vine Deloria Jr. and Indigenous studies scholars and activists to explain how place is sacred and how this is in sharp contrast to Christian fixation on time as sacred. I then explain settler colonialism and contrast it with Indigenous place relations. Building on this, I focus on agrarianism because it is central to Minnesota's ethos and economy. In the next section, "Radical Refusal and Recognition," I build on the work of

Coulthard, Betasamosake Simpson, Simpson, and other Indigenous studies scholars and discuss how in asserting the relationship to place at particular places and moments in which that relation is most threatened, Indigenous activists challenge and rework the terms of recognition. I argue that Indigenous activists' assertion of their relationship to place exposes and expels settler colonialist relations to place and reliance on linear time to assert that relationship. In the third and final section, "Imagining Place Relations Outside of Settler Colonial Logics," I illustrate how Indigenous activism makes visible and accessible ways to reimagine place and one's relationship with it outside of settler colonialist systems. I explain how Indigenous assertions of place and the rejection of Christian or colonialist time work to make Indigenous place relations visible and accessible. I close with what is at stake in seeing place through Indigenous eyes.

Contestations of Memory and Place

Memory places are those places that have been preserved, recreated, or constructed to contain and transmit specific memories which a collective holds to be important. These memory spaces compel visitors to think about a time and events other than that in which they presently exist.[21] Memory places like Gettysburg, Custer National Monument, or the Paul Wellstone Memorial mark the site of a major event and the people who participated in it. The designation of a physical space with a marker demarcates the space and/or the individuals or things named in that space as having significance. Written, visual, and/or aural messages convey the significance of the place. By designating a space and highlighting the events and people therein, the space contains and transmits the lessons or values attributed to the place, people, and events therein. The material and discursive elements within a site take on a meaning and significance beyond that which is otherwise immediately evident. The site of the Wellstone Memorial therefore is not simply a peaceful wooded site, but a place to remember, reinforce, and reenact the values Wellstone represented. Additionally, public messages about the site can be accessed via mediated texts such as websites and other transmittable public texts. People understand these places not only by visiting and interacting within the sites, but also through accessing what is published or posted about these sites. Memory spaces reflect a collectives' values back to them.

What a collective chooses to remember, via the preservation or reconstruction of a space, is an exercise and reflection of what it holds to be important or worth remembering. Memory sites bind memory and cultural values together and use historical people and/or events to represent and reinscribe these values. Memories are assemblages of the past that we use to help make sense of the past so as to navigate the present. "Collective memory," as communication scholar Barbie Zelizer explains, "are recollections that are instantiated beyond the individual by and for the collective."[22] Memory is critical to the construction, maintenance, and transformation of culture. In the collective process of determining which memories should be preserved, cultures identify and reaffirm their values. This process is unavoidably both inclusive and exclusive. In her examination of Israeli pioneer settlement museums, communication studies scholar Tamar Katriel explains, "history is affected and deflected by our persistent quest for memory."[23] Memory is inevitably incomplete and therefore contestable.[24]

The tensions over whose memories are worthy of public commemoration are evident in controversies over who and what should be remembered. When these memories are woven into places like state capitals, military forts, historical sites, and public art installations, they intimate these partial memories as complete.[25] Memories are not necessarily incorrect, but they are unavoidably incomplete. It is common, for example, to tell the story of the Homestead Act and land scrips opening up Minnesota to settlement by white male head of households while leaving out the story not only of land squatters, but also how Dakota, Ho-Chunk, and Ojibwe communities were already fishing, hunting, and farming this land.[26] It is more concise and convenient to narrow the story of the US-Dakota war to that of Dakota warriors and New Ulm defenders and not include treaties or Dakota and settler allies. I mean here to cast a critical eye onto what makes it into our collective history as well as the consequences of relying on linear logics of time.

Historical contexts are incapable of fully recognizing Indigeneity because Indigeneity rejects the distinction of the past from the present. Therefore, any site that embraces memory or history as distinction or a break from the present is inherently incapable of fully representing Indigenous peoples or Indigeneity.

Because linear time relies on the break between the past, present, and future, settler colonialism is incapable of fully recognizing Indigenous agency. Attempts to mark or affix Indigenous peoples in history, and then separate the past from the present and future, inherently fall short of fully representing Indigenous peoples and agency. Indigenous studies scholar Mishuana Goeman explains how Indigenous storytelling exposes and interrupts the linear narrative of past to present and asserts space over time. Goeman writes:

> [t]he dialectic of stories in the past and present break from the unidirectional, progressive narrative found in the narratives of manifest destiny. Indigenous conceptions of land are literally and figuratively the placeholder that moves through time and situates Indigenous knowledges. Conceiving of space as node rather than a linear time construct marked by supposed shifting ownerships is a powerful mechanism in resisting imperial geographies that order time and space in hierarchies and bury indigenous connections to place and anesthetize settler-colonial histories.[27]

Stories, knowledge, and lifeways that transcend and thereby expose time as an imposed settler colonial construct make visible and accessible Indigeneity. Unlike settler colonialism, Indigenous land relations do not rely on narratives of settlement to perpetually reinscribe itself. Indigenous place relations are not dependent upon logics of time and ownership. Time and ownership are interrelated as one codifies the other. Just as ownership is marked by terms and dates of transfer, dates define or index ownership. Indigenous land relations are defined by a relationship with land and with others who hold that relationship and thereby exist outside of settler colonial logics.

Place as Center

Place and maintaining a relationship with place, even when it is not physically accessible, is central to Indigeneity. Indigenous studies scholar Vine Deloria Jr. writes about land as the center of everything. The material and the spiritual world are one and the same. As Deloria Jr. explains, "[s]pace, . . . is determinative of the way that we experience things. . . . It is this unbroken connection that we have with the spirit world that will allow us to survive as a people."[28] Land is central to Indigenous being and understanding the world around them, their relations, and obligations. In his chapter, "Kinship with the world," Deloria Jr. explains, "[t]he simple proposition that Indians love nature and embrace it does not tell you why different tribes manifest their relationship to the land in different ways. If you talk to tribal peoples in those particular lands, you will get a better insight into why their religion and their culture developed in certain ways."[29] Religion and culture are grounded in the land, the place of tribal origin.

To understand the Indigenous culture and religion, one must see it as not just originated with the land, but inherently and completely connected to it. Explaining the "relationship between all things," decolonization scholar and activist Waziyatawin shares what "tuŋkaŋsida" means. Waziyatawin explained to historian Kelsey Carlson:

> The designation of a spiritual being among the Dakota differs from the designation often used by English speakers. For example, *tuŋkaŋsida, grandfather,* may apply to a human being or a number of human beings as a kinship term, but it is also applied to other spiritual beings. The term may refer to Wakaŋtaŋka (The Great Mystery), the rocks used in the sweat lodge, or the gigantic boulders that appear in our area of the country and whom the Dakota recognize as the oldest, most ancient beings.[30]

Waziyatawin's explanation conveys the complexity and interconnectedness between place and being, person and animal, material and spiritual. This particular language, culture, and relationship with the land is specific to the Dakota.

Dakota place relations, like other Indigenous nations, are accessible and evident via language and stories. In the first chapter of *Mni Sota Makoce: The Place of the Dakota*, authors Indigenous studies scholar Gwen Westerman and historian Bruce White explain the meaning of Mni Sota Makoce. Their book begins:

> [s]ixteen different verbs in the Dakota language describe returning home, coming home, or bringing something home. That is how important our homeplace is in Dakota regardless of where our history has taken us. No matter how far we go, we journey back home through language and songs and in stories our grandparents told us to share with our children.[31]

Westerman and White explain that in order to understand Minnesota as a Dakota place, one must understand and engage with Dakota land memories. They write, "to 'reclaim' Minnesota as a Dakota place is to once again interact with what is sacred and to recall its stories. We believe the place remembers, and as we walk near Minneopa Falls or in Blue Mound State Park or around [Lake Calhoun], we are surrounded by those memories held in the place."[32] Place holds stories, and being in place is not just how those stories are remembered but also how one interacts with the "sacred." Specific places hold Dakota knowledge, just as Dakota hold knowledge of these places. Interacting with spiritual sites as a Dakota is a way of practicing that knowledge. This knowledge and practice are central to Indigenous activism.

While the centrality of the land is universal to Indigenous peoples, the specifics of that relationship are unique to each tribal nation. Indigenous studies scholar Glen Coulthard cites Deloria Jr.'s argument that "American Indians hold their lands—places—as having the highest possible meaning, and all their statements made with this reference point in mind." Coulthard focuses on the idea that land is not simply the referent or that through which all meaning is derived, but rather land is the referent and referred. Discussing the centrality of land, Coulthard explains it as *a system of reciprocal relations and obligations* can teach us about living our lives in relation to one another and the natural world in nondominating and nonexploitative terms." The "relations and obligations" that are taught through ones' relationship with place are central to Indigenous being and specific to tribal nations. Calling this, "grounded normativity," Coulthard explains it as "the modalities of Indigenous land-connected practices and longstanding experiential knowledge that inform and structure our ethical engagements with the world and our relationships with human and nonhuman others over time."[33] Betasamosake Simpson explains Indigenous attachment to land. She writes, "[w]ithin Nishnaabeg thought, the opposite of dispossession is not possession, it is a deep, reciprocal, consensual *attachment*. Indigenous bodies don't relate to the land by possessing or owning it or having control over it. We relate to land through connection—generative, affirmative, complex, overlapping, and nonlinear *relationship*."[34] Grounded normativity is the academic term for Indigenous place-based systems of being and relating to the others and the world around oneself.

Building on Coulthard's work, Betasamosake Simpson explains what "grounded normativity" means as Indigenous ways of being. She explains:

> [t]he term itself is far less important in Indigenous circles; we've always known our way of life comes from the place or place through the practice of our modes of intelligence. We know that place includes place and waters, plants and animals, and the spiritual world—a peopled cosmos of influencing powers. We know that our practices code and reveal knowledge, and our knowledge codes and reveals practices.[35]

Betasamosake Simpson's words reveal the idea that being Indigenous or practicing Indigenous culture are connected. Her explanation, "our practices code and reveal knowledge, and our knowledge codes and reveals practices" reflects the importance of Indigenous practices because those practices reveal and renew culture. They are not a representation or semblance of culture, they are Indigenous culture.

Indigenous culture is maintained through communication practices such as ceremony, language, and storytelling. Goeman explicates how connections to place are maintained through communication and culture. She states:

> [t]hese rooted connections are the result of a relationship between place and people—they are not sacred because they are there, but rather they are imagined into being and spoken from generation to generation. They are carefully attended to through word and reconnected to through story and the act of remembering and caretaking.[36]

Story and remembering place are critical aspects of Indigeneity. As Indigenous studies scholars D. Anthony Tyeeme Clark and Malea Powell explain, "[t]he power of homescapes and the relational, therapeutic politics they generate are animated by stories, songs, and signs radiating outward from their many known and tended places as well as from the ceremonies human being perform within their boundaries."[37] Remembering via language and story, as well as remembering place by being there, are sacred.

Practicing Indigenous culture at the places of it is origin are critical. Culture is a reflection and reassertion of the power of place. Deloria Jr. and Indigenous studies scholar Daniel Wildcat explain, "[t]raditional American Indian cultural practices actively acknowledge and engage the power that permeates the many places recognized as sacred not by human proclamation or declaration, but by experience in those places."[38] Dakota children's presence, for example, at Bdote learning Dakota language and games, reflects the "sacred" of which Deloria Jr. and Wildcat speak. Bdote is the site of Dakota genesis and where the Minnesota and Mississippi rivers meet. Deloria Jr. explains, "[t]housands of years of occupancy on their lands taught tribal peoples the sacred landscapes for which they were responsible and gradually the structure of ceremonial reality became clear."[39] The practice of the Dakota language being spoken at the site and children learning and playing lacrosse brings the "ceremonial reality" of which Deloria Jr. speaks into being. Indigenous understanding of place as sacred is in stark contrast to Christian focus on time and marking events as sacred.

Fields of study such as anthropology and history and the ways they have informed communication studies rely on linear logics of time which thereby render history to the past. Colonialist logics of time are explained by biologist Stephen Jay Gould who states, "[a]t the end of the dichotomy—I shall call it time's arrow—history is an irreversible sequence of unrepeatable events. Each moment occupies its own distinct position in a temporal series, and all moments, considered in proper sequence, tell a story of linked events moving in a direction."[40] The dominance of chronos or linear time works to confine recognition of Indigenous people to the past. Cultural anthropologist Johannes Fabian explains the role of history in othering Indigenous peoples. Fabian states, "[i]t is by diagnosing anthropology's temporal discourse that one rediscovers the obvious, namely that there is no knowledge of the Other which is not also a temporal, historical, a political act."[41] Fabian contends that this imposed separation between the past and the present results in a differentiation between people and cultures of the past and the present. Marx argued that time is a measure of labor and therefore time is an economic measure.[42] Philosopher Henri Lefebvre, who draws on Marx, argues that time is imposed on place.[43] Finally, Deloria Jr. explicates the distinction between American Indian and Christian theological notions of time. He explains, "Christian theology has made a fetish of distinguishing between two modes of time, traditionally characterized as *kairos*, the fullness of time when qualitative experiences are present, and chronos, the mathematical time of clocks, seasons, and sequences."[44]

Central to Deloria Jr.'s conceptualization of space is the distinction between American Indian as "spatially located" and Christianity as "temporal." Deloria Jr. explains, "[t]he contrast between Christianity and its interpretation of history—the temporal dimension—and the American Indian tribal religions—basically spatially located—is clearly illustrated when we understand the nature of sacred mountains, sacred hills, sacred rivers, and other geographical features sacred to Indian tribes."[45] In Indigenous spirituality, the "mountains," "hills," and "rivers" are sacred. Time is irrelevant in Indigenous spirituality; in this way, the past, present, and future are always accessible. The focus on place makes these always and equally accessible. Indigeneity resists colonialist logics of place and time by asserting their relationship with place and insisting, for example, on the past as the present and the present as the past. As Indigenous studies scholar Nick Estes argues, "Indigenous notions of time consider the present to be structured entirely by our past and by our ancestors. There is no separation between the past, present and future, meaning that an alternative future is also determined by our understanding of our past."[46] Estes articulates the critical idea that not just are the past and present connected, but that "there is no separation between the past, present, and future." This is impossible to fully grasp if one remains couched in settler colonial logics that embrace time as linear or sequential.

Settler colonialism relies on linear logics of time which sequester Indigeneity and Indigenous peoples to the past. Historian Patrick Wolfe's oft-cited definition of settler colonialism emphasizes that "invasion is a structure and not an event." Wolfe explains, "negatively, [settler colonialism] strives for the dissolution of native societies. Positively, it erects a new colonial society on the expropriated land base—as I put it, settler colonizers come to stay: invasion is a structure not an event."[47] The structure of particular focus here is time, the separation and sequestering of the past from the present and future. The structures of settler colonialism, the systems and ideologies that fix the lifeways as well as the genocide of Indigenous peoples to the past, are what is most crucial. Indigenous peoples are always framed as pre-modern in contrast to settlers and settlement as modern.

Indigenous studies scholar J. Kēhaulani Kauanui explains "enduring Indigeneity" and "what it means to an understanding of settler colonialism." Kauanui uses settler colonialism to orientate her larger argument that "Indigenous peoples exist, resist, and persist; and that settler colonialism is a structure that endures indigeneity, as it holds out against it."[48] Settler colonialism "endures" and "holds out against" Indigeneity by constantly restating and reinstating itself. Indigeneity does not require this maintenance and therefore it "exist[s], resist[s], and persist[s]."

Indigenous peoples and land relations remain despite the continual [re] enactment of removal. In contrast, settler citizens and systems of settler colonialism require the constant [re]suturing onto place. As Kauanui explains, "the logic of elimination of the native is about the elimination of the native *as native*."[49] Indigenous peoples and communities hold out against settler colonialism which relies on their absorption or erasure as part of the dominant narrative of progress.

While I am mindful of how a focus on place risks further uptake of settler colonialist logics, I believe that a deep commitment to place and Indigenous analytics can work to expose these logics.[50] Place is central to both settler colonialism and Indigeneity. Indigenous studies scholars Eve Tuck and K. Wayne Yang state, "[w]ithin settler colonialism, the most important concern is place/ water/air/subterranean earth (place, for shorthand, in this article). Place is what is most valuable, contested, required."[51] Place is the currency by which identity is constituted. Our understanding of the places we hold most important is in part an understanding of ourselves. In writing about settlers and Indigenous peoples, Tuck and Yang write, "[o]ur/their relationships to land comprise our/ their epistemologies, ontologies, and cosmologies."[52] I argue that by centering this work on place we are able to not only examine the distinction between Indigenous relations of and with place and those of settler colonialism, but explicate and unsettle settler colonialist logics.

Land as a means of constituting identity, particularly as it intersects with nationalist and white agrarian identities, is central to settler colonialism. Settler colonialism illuminates an important way in which place constitutes identity.[53] The idea that white settlers hold a unique and superior right to land is grounded in the ideology of whiteness as a civilizing force. The frontier myth has origins in the work of historian Frederick Jackson Turner who argued that the United States' "national customs and character" and "success as a people" was a result of the nation's experience on the frontier.[54] The power of the frontier myth is that it provides a narration and justification for settlement and, in doing so, imbricates individuals as agents not only of the original settlement but also as guardians of it in the contemporary moment. Settlement becomes not simply the means to establish citizenship and nationhood, but a matter of its maintenance and defense. In his discussion of the "myth of the frontier," historian Richard Slotkin explains how the frontier myth was used to justify oppression, noting that "the conquest of the wilderness and the subjugation or displacement of the Indigenous peoples who originally inhabited it have been the means to our achievement of national identity, a democratic polity, an ever-expanding economy, and a phenomenally dynamic and 'progressive' civilization."[55]

Owning and farming land has long been a means of establishing not just U.S. citizenship, but Godliness. The Lockean virtues of land ownership are coded as citizenship.[56] The idea that the cultivation of land as a means to ownership and citizenship is echoed in Jeffersonian and Jacksonian land logics. Sociology scholar Michael Schudson explains how "the virtues of the farmer—independence, self-sufficiency, a permanent commitment to the community, and a high regard for protecting the same virtues in others—were also the virtues of the citizen."[57] Jefferson wrote, "[t]hose who labour in the earth are the chosen people of God, if ever He had a chosen people, whose breasts He has made His peculiar deposit for substantial and genuine virtue."[58]

The most consequential U.S. philosophical and legal ideologies are grounded in racism. The Doctrine of Discovery, originated in the 1493 papal bull "Inter Caetera," directed explorers to claim, colonize, and convert any place and peoples they encounter. This doctrine was codified into U.S. land laws via the 1823 Supreme Court case *Johnson v. McIntosh* (21 U.S. 543). Chief Justice John Marshall grounded his argument in the Discovery Doctrine, writing "discovery gave title to the government, by whose subjects, or by whose authority, [the discovery] was made, against all other European governments."[59] It was this and subsequent court decisions that have reaffirmed the legal standing of Indigenous nations as having rights of occupation, though not dominion. The Supreme Court has repeatedly stripped Indigenous nations and peoples of their sovereignty. The racism that informed the many decisions continues into the present. In his examination of those Supreme Court decisions most influential on Indigenous American rights, Indigenous and legal scholar Robert Williams Jr. examines the Rehnquist decision in 1978 Supreme Court case *Oliphant v. Suquamish Indian Tribe* (435 U.S. 191) and assesses that much of the nineteenth century legal documents Rehnquist draws on "consistently and unembarrassedly stereotypes Indians as lawless, uncivilized, unsophisticated, warlike savages."[60] These philosophical, religious, and legal arguments are the premise to some of the most consequential land laws in U.S. history.

Together, the Homestead and Dawe's Acts resulted in mass settlement and the mass removal and break up of Indigenous reservations and communities. The 1862 Homestead Act is perhaps most recognized for its role in dividing and deeding land to millions of settlers.[61] The Dawe's Act, or what is known as "checkerboarding," broke the collective culture and land management of tribal nations and required Indigenous Americans to farm their individual plots.[62] Together, these two land laws took over 420 million acres from Indigenous peoples.[63] Judicial precedence around property rights informs cases related to land and religious freedom.

Place as property, and not as sacred or tied to culture, dominates U.S. legal code. In his analysis of the Chimney Rock case (*Lyng v. Northwest Indian Cemetery Protective Association*, 485 U.S. 439), legal scholar Howard Vogel explains the "power of the Anglo-American view of place as property, subject to title and possession, as an important feature of the American narrative embraced by most European Americans, against the meaning of place within Native American narratives."[64] Settler logics of place dominate Indigenous place logics. Drawing on the work of Vine Deloria Jr. legal scholar Robert Nichols develops the idea of "negative property rights." Nichols explains how "to claim property in something is, in effect, to construct a relationship with others, namely, a relationship of exclusion."[65] Claiming or possessing a place, and the forced removal of Indigenous place relations, is a way of being and belonging in settler colonialism.

Participating in "settler society" through occupying places and/or participating in other systems engendered and reinforced through that occupation of place is a way of thus constituting citizenship. As Wolfe states, settlers "are made in the dispossessing, a ceaseless obligation that has to be maintained across generations if the Natives are not to come back. Along with the place, then, come identity, selfhood, family, belonging, all the qualities that make us fight."[66] Indigenous peoples are often still a part of settler colonialist narratives, but only at the point of disappearing. "Playing Indian," as Indigenous scholar Philip J. Deloria explains, allowed white Americans to use Indigenous identities or caricatures as part of the larger project of making settlers. As Deloria explains, "[f]rom the very beginning, Indian-white relations and Indian play itself have modeled a characteristically American kind of domination in which the exercise of power was hidden, denied, qualified, or mourned."[67] In this way, their perpetual removal is put in service to the more dominant narrative of settlement and nation-building.[68] Indigenous studies scholar Kevin Bruyneel explains that settler memory is "a mode of collective memory that places

Indigeneity in the background of race and other political discussions in the United States by simultaneously remembering and disavowing, seeing and not seeing, marking as both present and absent Indigenous people and the history of colonialism."[69] As historian Adam J. Barker explains, settler colonialism is "the power to displace, the privilege to forget."[70] The disappearing Indigenous person is prominent part of the narrative of settlement and nation building. From manifest destiny to farming the heartland, the frontier is central to settler colonialism, particularly here in Minnesota.[71]

It is not any stretch to say that Minnesota has been, since its inception to the present moment, an agrarian-focused state. From the Grange Movement of the 1860s and 70s, to the Democratic Farm Labor movement of the 1910s to 1940s, the farm crisis of the 1980s, to contemporary farming, Minnesota is economically, politically, and culturally grounded in agriculture.[72] In May 2023 the Minnesota Department of Agriculture website stated, "Minnesota's combined agriculture, food processing, and forestry industries contribute over 15% of Minnesota's total economic activities and support over 10% of all jobs."[73] According to the U.S. Department of Agriculture 2017 census, Minnesota ranked first in grain sales, second in hog sales, and fourth in dairy sales. According Minnesota Public Radio, cropland takes up more than 75 percent of the state.[74] Not only is farming a central part of the state economy, but it is also a prominent part of the state ethos. It is within this context that Indigenous claims to being must assert themselves.

Radical Refusal and Recognition

At stake is the larger question of how Indigenous activists negotiate making claims to sovereignty within the epistemological and, often, legal context of non-Indigenous government bodies.[75] Indigenous arguments for existence, therefore, seek the same ends, recognition and sovereignty. But the terms that it relies on, and thereby risk reifying, are what is at stake. The challenge, here, is how "Indianness" is articulated, how Indigenous peoples "talk back" within and through systems which are imbued with settler colonialism. Historian Frederick Hoxie explains how Charles Eastman (Dakota) and his colleagues talk back to American civilization, challenging its guiding ideologies and the brutal impact they had on Native Americans. Eastman and others, as Hoxie explains:

> articulated a vision of Native American culture that inspired persistence in Indian communities across the nation while laying the foundations for cultural revivals that would take place in ensuing decades. By talking back to civilization, Eastman's generation helped define, preserve, and even stimulate faith in "Indianness" for the remainder of the twentieth century.[76]

In his vast writing, Eastman made accessible the grounded normativity, or Dakota lifeways, that he and his community still enact. Centering analysis of Indigenous claims to being in Indigenous epistemologies is therefore crucial.

Asserting and practicing grounded normativity, in the face of and despite settler colonialism systems and institutions, is a form of activism. Central to Indigenous activism is a turning away from settler colonialist systems and a self-recognition of Indigeneity on one's own terms. Drawing on Hegel and Fanon, Coulthard argues that instead of seeking recognition from the settler state, Indigenous activists in First Nation turn away from state recognition as a means to emancipation and instead turn inward. Coulthard argues for:

> a politics that is less orientated around attaining an affirmative form of recognition from the settler-state and society and more about critically evaluating, reconstructing and redeploying culture and tradition in ways that seek to prefigure, alongside those with similar ethical commitments, a radical alternative to the structural and psycho-affective facets of colonial domination.[77]

The collection of activism in this book reflects the "reconstructing and redeploying of culture and tradition" of which Coulthard speaks.

Grounded normativity is the root of Indigenous sovereignty and refusal. Betasamosake Simpson explains, "I use the term interchangeably with Nishnaabeg intelligence, like Coulthard, as a strategic intervention into how the colonial world and the academy position, construct, contain, and shrink Indigenous knowledge systems." Refusal is evident in how Indigenous individuals and communities live. Writing about "kwe" as it "recognizes a spectrum of gender expressions [that] exist in embedded in grounded normativity,"

Betasamosake Simpson explains that "refusal is an appropriate response to oppression, and within this context it is always generative, that is, it is always living the alternative."[78] Refusal is evident in the insistence and subsistence of living Indigenous sovereignty in one's own life and in relation with others.

Refusal is a way of constituting Indigeneity on and for its own terms. Simpson builds on Coulthard's work and explains, "refusal rather than recognition is an option for producing and maintaining alternative structures of thought, politics, and traditions away from and in critical relationship to states."[79] Writing about the Kahnawà:ke Mohawks as a "cartography of refusal," Simpson argues that the cases she explores "demonstrate the fundamentally interrupted and interruptive capacity of that life within settler society." Simpson examines how by living Indigenous lifeways, the Kahnawà:ke "interrupt and fundamentally challenge stories that have been told about them and about others like them, as the structure of settlement that strangles their political form and tries to take their land and selves from them."[80] Living as an Indigenous person with a deep love of and connection to land is central to refusal and resistance. Betasamosake Simpson explains the "intense love of land, of family, and of our nations that has always been the spine of Indigenous resistance." She continues, "we need to join together in a rebellion of love, persistence, commitment, and profound caring and create constellations of coresistance, working together toward a radical alternative present based on deep reciprocity and the gorgeous generative refusal of colonial recognition."[81]

Betasamosake Simpson explains what she means by "resurgence" and why she attaches "radical" to it. "Resurgence," she says, is needed to distinguish it as "a lens, critical analysis, a set of theoretical understandings and organizing and mobilizing platform [that] has the potential to wonderfully transform life on Turtle Island." The inclusion of "radical" and "resurgence" is a reflection of her "taking back of resurgence from the realm of neoliberalism and reclaiming its revolutionary potential." Betasamosake Simpson explicates Coulthard's and Simpson's work and argues that radical resurgence is made up of "a refusal of state recognition as an organizing platform and mechanism for dismantling the systems of colonial domination" and refusal of "the state's framing of the issues we organize around and respond to and re-embed these issues within Indigenous political contexts and realities and within the place of productive refusal as a mechanism for building unity within the struggle."[82] It is the type of “interruptions” and “refusals” that Simpson writes about that I examine in these case studies.

Refusing to be hailed or interpreted through settler colonial logics creates a productive space in which Indigenous logics are made visible. Writing on the politics of recognition and refusal, Simpson explores “the generative alternative that refusal may play not only as a political practice but as a mode of analysis.”[83] Simpson’s words convey the idea that analysis of Indigenous places, via any other epistemology or methodological lens, will inevitably leave gaps in terms of recognition. Writing about the significance of the Kahnawà:ke lacrosse team passports being recognized for international travel, Simpson explains what is at stake. She writes, “[t]here is more than one political show in town. If a Haudenosaunee person is to travel internationally, for example, on a Confederacy passport, then the very boundaries and lawfulness of the original territorial referent is called into question.”[84] Seizing these moments in which the “territorial referent” can be “called into question” is a tactic of refusal. Refusal is not simply a denial of the terms of recognition, it is a demand to set these terms.

Refusal opens up another way for thinking about the relationship between recognition and justice work. Refusal challenges the terms of recognition and justice insofar as they function as governing logics. Simpson explains, “[r]efusal is a symptom, a practice, a possibility for doing things differently, for thinking beyond the recognition paradigm that is the agreed upon ‘antidote’ for rendering justice in deeply unequal scenes of articulation.”[85] Refusal interrupts liberal recognition terms and asserts Indigeneity outside of them. Echoing grounded normativity, Simpson argues, “[o]ur elders and Knowledge Holders have always put great emphasis into how things are done. This reinforces the idea that it is our own tools, strategies, values, processes and intellect that are going to build our new house.”[86] Following Simpson’s argument, understanding Indigenous being and claims to belonging requires recognizing these claims to being as both reflective and constitutive of Indigenous logics.

An important part of grounded normativity is that, as an ontology, it also reconfigures the ways in which mobility is constitutive and reflective of Indigenous activism. It is possible, for example, to critique the role of the federal government in the 1954 Relocation Act and other state-imposed dislocation of Indigenous peoples and at the same time recognize that this forced mobility can inform inter-tribal resistance. Building on the work of Goeman and Betasamosake Simpson, these case studies demonstrate how intertribal mobility can be understood as intertribal Indigenous constellations that reflect grounded normativity and Indigenous resistance. Betasamosake Simpson explains how she sees mobility in four ways. She explains it exists "within grounded normativity as an embedded Indigenous practice, mobility as a response to colonial resistance, mobility as deliberate and strategic resurgence, and mobility as direct or indirect forced expulsion, relocation, and displacement and the creation of Indigenous diaspora."[87] Mobility can be a "response to colonial resistance" as well as a "deliberate and strategic resurgence." All of these aspects of mobility are evident in these case studies.

Imagining Place Relations outside of Settler Colonialism

Centering this discussion on Indigenous logics or epistemologies of place allows one to think about one's relationship to it outside of the settler colonialist terms of ownership or linear logics of time. In doing so, we recognize the role that ownership plays in constituting and limiting the terms of being and belonging. It is, as historian Lorenzo Veracini explains, to rethink the "grammar of sovereignty."[88] Being presented with ways to relate to place that are not premised or dependent upon ownership raises the question of how place and one's relationship to it can otherwise be constituted.

What happens to our ability to orientate ourselves in place when the map and figurative or literal fence posts we use to orientate ourselves no longer suffice? This might be akin to navigating a place by its waterways instead of its highways or its prairies instead of its plat maps. Indigenous studies scholar Jodi Byrd argues that centering discussions on place can illuminate the ways in which belonging and relating are constructed and circumscribed. Byrd argues that a deep focus on place, "with its own animate and deep planetary remembrances, might provide avenues of return to intercede against the enforced dismemberments and dis/possessions that have shaped Atlantic worlds."[89] Seeing and interrogating the logics of belonging through possessing makes other ways of being and belonging, those evident via a place's "animate and deep planetary remembrances," much more visible.

This requires not only seeing the logics of possession, but examining how each of our own connections to place are constructed, maintained, and circumscribed through logics of possession. Indigenous studies scholar Kim Tall Bear writes about the challenges of "settler kinship." Drawing on the work of Sisseton Wahpeton Dakota artist and teacher Gabrielle Tateyuskanskan, Tall Bear writes, "[m]aking kin can call non-Indigenous people (including those who don't fit easily into the 'settler' category) to be more accountable to [I]ndigenous peoples and understand their own relations with place."[90] Recognizing Indigenous relations to place opens up recognition of the role of political, economic, and social institutions in setting the terms of being and belonging. It makes visible how narratives of place imbricate settler farmer citizens.

This deep focus on land through Indigenous eyes is a horizon to not only understanding land but each other. Coulthard argues that what Deloria Jr. is attempting to do is more than just articulating the significance of the relationship that Indigenous peoples hold with their land. Coulthard writes, Deloria "is attempting to explicate the position that land occupies as an ontological framework for understanding relationships." Indigenous land relations stand apart from and makes settler colonialist land relations visible and open to interrogation. Coulthard continues, "[p]lace is a way of knowing, of experiencing and relating to the world and with others; and sometimes these relational practices and forms of knowledge guide forms of resistance against other rationalizations of the world that threaten to destroy or replace our senses of place."[91] It is through a deep attention to place that the logics dependent on time and possession can be exposed and different land relations imagined.

What is at stake is more fully seeing our relations to place and to each other. Taking Indigenous place analytics to heart requires relinquishing the privilege that is derived from using settler colonialist place logics as the terms of belonging. Writing about Indigenous justice in Canada, Indigenous studies scholar Taiaiake Alfred explains what "radical imagination" requires. He states, "[r]adical imagination is reenvisioning your existence on this place without the inherited privileges of conquest and empire. It is accepting the fact of a meaningful prior Indigenous presence and taking action to support struggles not only of social and economic justice, but political justice for Indigenous nations as well."[92] Indigenous and communications studies scholar Na'puti explains her work in "remapping," as that which "considers place in creative and dynamic connections with place and ocean, providing a more expansive register of connections with and beyond landcentric configurations of space and time."[93] In her work theorizing an "oceanic orientation in communication studies," Na'puti explains that it "insists upon the centrality of Indigenous subjects to the ocean, islands, atolls, and archipelagos—orientating our research to attend to peoples' experiences as interconnected exchanges and kinships that belong to these places."[94] In attending to those understandings of place that have been largely silenced, we are able to recognize that there is more than a single story or truth about a place.

This project seeks to dwell for a bit on the ghosts of the past-present-future and who therefore exist outside of stories of states and land scrips. As Simpson closes her afterword to the series "Whither Settler Colonialism?" in *Settler Colonial Studies*:

> [a]nd in time with the attention to time, to its relationship to that which is beyond our sense of the "real"—nation-states, their narration of truth, of sturdiness, of fixidity, of their claim on what is really "real"—these essays have documented, analyzed, and theorized from a base that acknowledges and affirms a settler colonial project, but with nuanced attention to specificities, struggles, to the ghosts in the machine.[95]

The examples I examine in this book reflect an assertion of Indigenous being and relation to place, the ways in which these assertions challenge and rework the terms of recognition and via that refusal, generate and make Indigeneity visible.

In chapter one, "Indigenous Refusal and Rejecting Genocide," I explore how Indigenous activists' response to the Minneapolis Walker Arts Center's *Scaffold* reflected an intertribal mobility and rejection of settler colonial logics. *Scaffold* was planned to be an outdoor art installation at the Minneapolis Sculpture Garden of a to-scale replica of the scaffold used to execute 38+2 Dakota men after the U.S.-Dakota war, the largest state-sponsored execution in the history of the United States. Three Rivers Park, formerly Murphy's Landing, features a historic settlers' village located in Shakopee, a community twenty miles from Minneapolis. I examine the discursive, visual, and performative elements of each site as well as published news sources and websites. In my examination of *Scaffold* and The Landing, I assess both how settler colonialism is enacted in these networked spaces and how Indigenous activism reflected a rejection of settler colonial logics and enacted grounded normativity.

In chapter two, "Reparative Justice and Interventions in Settler Nostalgia," I examine how Makoce Ikikcupi, a reparative justice land return project, directs its appeals for funding to settler descendants and how these appeals intersect with and make visible the role of nostalgia for the family farm and the disappearing Indigenous. To get at these discourses, I examine a collection of newspaper articles covering Minnesota Farm Bureau sesquicentennial and centennial award–winning family farms from 2000 to 2020. Along with this, I examine the Makoce Ikikcupi website and newspaper coverage. By analyzing these two different sets of discourses about place, I cast into sharper relief the ways in which settler relations with place are constructed and circumscribed by state logics of possession and linear time. I argue that the assertion of Dakota lifeways via Makoce Ikikcupi reflects a negotiation of the terms of recognition. Settler land relations are marshalled into arguments for the financial support of Dakota lifeways as a form of reparative justice for the forced expulsion of Dakota from the state.

In chapter three, "Dakota Memory Maps and Re-Membering the Land," I examine Historic Fort Snelling at Bdote and the ways in which Indigenous terms of belonging are visible and accessible as well as how the demarcation of the site through signs, maps, and trails reveals how settler colonial narratives of time are sutured into place. I analyze the built and rebuilt structures, signs, and website and argue that the site makes visible Dakota terms of refusal. The signage and cacophony of literal and bureaucratic paths and demarcations makes visible the tenuousness of institutional claims to place. Dakota references and significations of the site stand out in sharp contrast for the ways they articulate Dakota connection to this site outside of settler colonial logics. Indigenous refusal as generative is evident in the ways in which Dakota refusal to have themselves and their relationship to the site defined and delineated within these state logics.

In the conclusion, I recap the centrality of land to the Indigenous concept of grounded normativity and settler colonialism. I argue that, by examining settler colonialist logics through grounded normativity and Indigenous logics of refusal, the ways in which settler colonialism has to constantly reinscribe itself via timelines and built spaces is made visible. In contrast, Indigeneity exists outside of and irrespective of these narratives. I discuss the tensions inherent in the work of Indigeneity to make itself known through settler colonialist logics and how activists seize on and rework these into Indigenous terms of recognition. Next, I review how these studies of Indigenous activism make visible how land relations are central to Indigenous existence and resistance.

I close with discussion of the implications of this examination for the field of contemporary rhetorical studies and Indigenous studies.

My Own Positionality

The risk of replicating the very systems responsible for that which the critic seeks to uproot is real. Colonialism scholar Linda Tuhiwai Smith challenges non-Indigenous scholars to recognize the ways in which the dominant paradigms of research are premised on the othering of Indigenous peoples and sees "research as a significant site of struggle between the interests and way of knowing of the West and the interests and ways of resisting of the Other." Scholars, particularly non-Indigenous scholars like myself, must be attentive to not only the ways in which their work may perpetuate settler colonialism but also the ways in which they benefit from such perpetuities. Tuhiwai Smith writes, "research is not an innocent or distant academic exercise but an activity that has something at stake and that occurs in a set of political and social conditions."[96] While studies in decoloniality are attentive to this, non-Indigenous scholars' increasing participating in Indigenous studies makes the need particularly urgent.[97] It is in this spirit that I offer what follows as a matter of what guides this work and what might guide others' reading of it.

Studies of settler colonialism, particularly those carried out by settler descendants, carry a number of inherent risks. I am a settler descendent attempting to do the work of decolonization.[98] Tuhiwai Smith explains "the white settler reasserts her or his power through self-reflection" and "[i]n doing so, his or her subjectivity is reaffirmed against the foil of the 'oppressed' people who still remain 'affectable' others [e.g., Indigenous peoples and people of color] who provide the occasion for this self-reflection."[99] As Smith and other Indigenous scholars argue, studies in settler colonialism become simply matters of resettlement.[100] Intercultural scholar Paulette Regan, who examines the Truth and Reconciliation Commission work in Canada, explains how restorative justice efforts can be undermined by a "singular focus on the Other [which] blinds us from seeing how settler history, myth, and identity have shaped and continue to shape our attitudes in highly problematic ways. It prevents us from acknowledging our own need to decolonize"[101] Unavoidably though, this examination risks recentering settler colonialism.

I take these risks quite seriously and it is therefore why it is important to be to be clear and succinct about my own positionality. My identity as a fifth- and third-generation Irish and Norwegian farming family is quite evident. My family name is on the 1898 plat maps framed on my office wall and at the head of our clan when we march on Saint Patrick's Day. When I drive by the home place, I remember the outbuildings and fields that constituted my world growing up. I think about land in terms of memories of walking beans (so many rows), picking rocks (so many rocks), and the life it afforded my family then and now. I know that the land became my families not only through hard work, but through land scrips and other legal avenues—all of which fall within the logics of ownership. I know land scrips were preceded by preemption, treaties, and wars; that one enabled the other. I see the home place two ways now.

It is a dialectics of place that I propose though which centers Indigenous epistemologies. Critical thinking is about holding two, sometimes competing, thoughts. I can see the land through my own eyes and how the systems that define and regulate it benefit my family and me. I can also see the land through Indigenous eyes and how those very same systems harm Dakota communities and culture. My focus, as a communication scholar, is how the systems of ownership are taken up and reiterated through revered historical places and discourses about those places. I am interested in how place tells a story about and to a community. When the stories of and systems of settlement are held up as the only story or way of relating to land and each other, we all lose something. I think that if we are all truly interested in and committed to these places and the communities that share them, then why wouldn't we want to understand them more deeply? For non-Indigenous folks, this requires seeing these places through Indigenous eyes, through the relations that are not dependent upon logics of ownership but of relationships with the land.

CHAPTER ONE

Indigenous Refusal and Rejecting Genocide

This is a painful part of history for our Dakota people which includes the overt acts of genocide directed at our people, not something to be depicted in a sculpture garden next to a giant rooster or spoon with a cherry.

—Cheyanne St. John (Lower Sioux), statement on Durant's *Scaffold*

In May of 2017, a curious sight began to take shape on the Minneapolis skyline. The highly anticipated one-year renovation of the eleven-acre Minneapolis Sculpture Garden, located at the Walker Art Center and managed by the Walker Art Center and the Minneapolis Park and Recreation Board, was nearly complete. Situated in the heart of Minneapolis, the largest urban sculpture garden and one of the most celebrated parks in the country, the Minneapolis Sculpture Garden is a popular attraction for both residents and visitors.[1] As the opening weekend approached, and the final installations took shape around the iconic installation that elevated the site to national prominence—*Spoonbridge and Cherry*—one piece was met with astonishment and outrage.[2] *Scaffold* was the life-size replica of the gallows used in the December 26, 1862, mass execution of 38 Dakota men in Mankato, Minnesota.[3]

There are a number of resources helpful to understanding the execution and the events leading up to it. The documentary, *Dakota 38*, details a commemorative ride which begins in Flandreau, SD and ends at Reconciliation Park in Mankato, MN, the site of the execution. The ride originated in the dream of

Dakota elder Jim Miller who had no knowledge of the execution and went on to lead it for years beginning in 2005.[4] While this ride is arguably the most notable in Indigenous and non-Indigenous press, other commemorations focused on women and youth are also held. Beginning in 1986, a seventy-one-mile commemorative run from Fort Snelling to Reconciliation Park has been held.[5] Finally, a 150-mile march led by Dakota women begins at Lower Sioux and ends at Fort Snelling, following the same path that Dakota women, children, and elders were forced to march in November 1862.[6] For Dakota, other Indigenous peoples, and non-Indigenous people who know Dakota history, the memory of 1862 is alive. This is in stark contrast to those who do not know U.S.-Dakota history.

By using Dakota genocide as artistic fodder, *Scaffold* invited visitors to playfully engage the issue of state-sponsored genocide without having to contemplate its implications.[7] In her *City Pages* article, "Genocide and Mini-Golf in the Minneapolis Sculpture Garden," local artist Ashley Fairbanks articulates the outrage and pain many felt over *Scaffold*. Fairbanks explains the ways in which the structure echoed the memory of the 38 Dakota men hanged as well as that of Little Crow (Taoyateduta), a Dakota leader, whose scalp and partial remains were prominently displayed in the Minnesota state capital for years.[8]

> It was the mockup of kids playing on it that got me.
>
> The language comparing it to a play structure. White folks having a great day on a gallows designed to evoke the exact imagery from the largest mass execution in U.S. history. White folks whose great-greats stood and cheered as those 38 men hung, who went to see Little Crow's remains on display. Now taking selfies on this evil structure.
>
> Their children running up and down the stairs, stairs just like the ones that 38 Dakota men ascended, singing, and never came back down.[9]

As Fairbanks notes, there was one discernable difference between the 1862 structure and the Walker Art Center's *Scaffold*. Just like the other installations in the Minneapolis Sculpture Garden, which are designed to be interactive, *Scaffold* included at least three stairways ascending to a platform complete with hand railings so that, as she says, "white folks" can have "a great day on a gallows." *Scaffold* at the Sculpture Garden was one of several representations of the people and events of the settlement era in Minnesota. One of the most prominent representations of the settlement era is The Landing, an eighty-eight-acre settlers village made up of authentic family homes from the 1840s to the 1890s curated from the surrounding area and relocated to the area around Indian Agent Richard Murphy's trading post and inn located just forty miles south of the Minneapolis Sculpture Garden in Shakopee, Minnesota.

Scaffold and The Landing both represent the Dakota community but limit that representation to moments of genocide and imminent removal. The Landing is a curated assemblage of authentic family homes, farms, and businesses relocated from within the Minnesota River Valley.[10] Murphy's Inn, the site's original namesake until its renaming in 2008, is the only structure authentic to the site.[11] Prior to building the inn in 1858, Richard Murphy was an Indian Agent at Fort Snelling just twenty miles north (1848–1849).[12] It was Ṡakṗe's village that brought the businessman Murphy, as well as trader and farmer Oliver Faribault in 1839 and ministers Samuel and Gideon Pond in 1847, to the area. Faribault's trader's cabin was moved the short distance away to just a hundred feet or so from the ruins of Murphy's Inn and the ruins of the Pond cabin are just outside of the site and marked with a state historical marker. Ṡakṗe's band was there until about 1830 when they moved to the north side of the river, just across from Murphy's Inn and ferry landing. This band and other Dakota tribes lived there until the 1840s when they were pushed further west. The Landing is in the community of Shakopee, named after Ṡakṗe, who was a Dakota chief who died in 1860. His son, an elder in 1862, was one of the leaders who was consulted in the decision to engage in the U.S.-Dakota war. After the war, Ṡakṗe escaped to Canada where two years later he was captured and taken to Fort Snelling with Wakan Ożaŋżaŋ (Medicine Bottle).[13] The two were hanged at Fort Snelling in November 1865.[14] The moniker "38+2" is a reference to the 38 men hanged in the mass execution and Ṡakṗe and Wakan Ożaŋżaŋ. The Landing is twenty miles south of the Minneapolis Sculpture Garden and forty miles north of Reconciliation Park, the site of the hanging, in Mankato.[15]

Interpreting *Scaffold* and The Landing in relation to each other offers unique insight into how settler colonialism relies on representations of the disappearance of Indigenous peoples as well as how Indigenous activists challenge these representations by asserting Indigenous epistemologies of place. Activists used the site of the installation to expose and challenge representations of Dakota as they served as part of a larger narrative of the state and asserted their relation to this place outside of settler colonialist terms of belonging. Part of the ways in which settler colonial logics function is to include representations of Indigenous peoples and to do so in such a way that these representations serve the greater narrative of colonialism.[16] Inclusion of the mass execution of the 38+2 Dakota men reflects this insofar as Indigenous people are included in the historical narrative and contemporary landscape, but only at the point of their execution and exodus. The activists named the 38+2 and, in doing so, asserted the past in the present and the future. Through their signage, their consistent presence, and their invitation to engage in discussion outside at the site and inside working with the Walker, activists exercised a sort of rhetorical seizure of the site. The activists asserted Indigenous logics of time and the unbreakable connection to place and rejected the terms of recognition offered by *Scaffold* and the Walker.

I begin discussion by explaining how settler colonialist notions of time and place are different from Indigenous focus on place. I then examine the built spaces, structures, paths, and signs at The Landing and how this curated assemblage of the past represents the escalating pace of settlement and the ways in which Indigeneity is present but only in a sort of ephemeral sense. I examine the site, too, in the broader geographical and socio-economic context. With The Landing being at the site of Ṡakṗe's village and just a few miles from Mystic Lake Casino, the site and nearby surrounding area reflect the implications of historic as well as contemporary dislocation for the Dakota. Next, I explore the rapid and sustained response of activists as *Scaffold* literally emerged on the Minneapolis landscape. I examine the responses by the Walker and the artist as well. After this, I discuss the 2022 opening of Dakota artist Angela Two Stars's work *Okciyapi* in the Walker Sculpture Garden as a response by the Walker to the outcry over *Scaffold*. Finally, I close with a developing project, the Shakopee Riverfront Cultural Trail, a collaborative effort with multiple municipal entities and the Shakopee Mdewakanton community which will build a 2.5-mile trail along the Minnesota River and through The Landing. I begin by examining The Landing and argue that as a sort of redacted story of the site, it makes possible a benign narrative of nineteenth-century settlement.

Contingencies of Settlement

The organization of The Landing makes visible the sort of schizophrenia of space and time in which settler land logics require continual resettlement. Settler colonialist notions of time as linear are visible in the timeline of settlement told at The Landing. Paleontologist Stephen Gould's explanation of "time's arrow" is evident in the arrangement of buildings at The Landing. As the era moves from the fur trade into settlement, there is less space between the structures. There is, then, less and less space to presumably see the Dakota connection to land. Yet, read through Vine Deloria Jr.'s explanation of "the unbroken connection" Dakota connection to land and that connection's role as ever present, Dakota connection to land is always present. Inversely, it is the settler narrative of time that must constantly reassert itself through its retelling. Reflective of Coulthard's explanation of grounded normativity, Indigenous relations with place are ever present; they do not require a continual reenactment or resettlement.

The response to *Scaffold* is an assertion of the constant relationship with place and rejection of settler colonialist time. The continual presence of activists at the site of the *Scaffold* reflected an assertion of Indigenous time. While settler colonialism framed 1862 as in the past and thereby sequestered from the present, Indigenous activists rejected this. The activists at the site demanded that the past, present, and future be present and accessible. The presence of activists and signage by different ages reflected Indigenous studies scholar J. Kēhaulani Kauanui's argument of "enduring Indigeneity."[17] *Scaffold* constituted Indigenous peoples as inanimate, their agency confined to the past. The activists, though, constituted Indigenous peoples as animate, their agency in the present, as well as the past and future. The activists' presence and larger response pushed back against the force of the *Scaffold* as it reflected an attempt to fold the past into a larger narrative of place and time. Any shock over the construction of *Scaffold* is quickly mitigated when the one considers the ubiquitousness of settler nostalgia in the area.

The Landing is an anesthetized and abbreviated version of the nineteenth-century Minnesota River Valley in which the removal of the Dakota is folded into the larger narrative of settlement. The arrangement of the structures around the crumbling foundation of Indian agent and state senator Richard Murphy's inn centers Murphy as pivotal not only to the ostensible "development" of the Minnesota River Valley, but also the state. Moving through the site, visitors engage in a participatory enactment of white settlement starting with the fur trade, to farmer settlers, and finally to urban commerce. The site, as well as special events it hosts, like "Little House on the River Camp," invokes and reifies nineteenth-century settlement and twenty-first century silences.

Although the renaming of the site in 2008, from the longtime Murphy's Landing to The Landing, was intended to open it up to a broader interpretation, the site's layout and structures overwhelm this potential.

As a sort of mythological representation of nineteenth-century Minnesota, The Landing eschews critical examination of the economic and cultural tensions of the era. Indian Agent Richard Murphy's inn, the only building original to the site, is surrounded by structures that are not original to the land upon which they now sit. Murphy is framed as an innkeeper, a perspective that positions him as an icon of economic and civic development rather than as an Indian agent to the Dakota. Another celebrated structure on the site is the Oliver Faribault cabin, which, like the other structures on the site, is authentic though relocated from the surrounding area.[18] Similar to Murphy, Faribault's role as fur trader is highlighted over that of government interpreter at the 1851 treaties.[19] This excised version of nineteenth-century settlement obscures the role that Indian agents and fur traders played in engineering not only the settlement of the area but the removal of Dakota. A more complete recounting of Murphy and Faribault, perhaps from a Dakota perspective, would render a more complex account of the settlement era and the site. The abridged version of the nineteenth-century Minnesota River Valley offered via The Landing works to continuously resettle the Minnesota River Valley in such a way in that one need not contemplate the ways in Dakota existed and exist here.

The ease of movement enabled by the walking path and the layout of the buildings creates a sense of cohesiveness and comprehensiveness. The arrangement of the buildings and walking paths encourage visitors to begin at the 1830s Faribault cabin and end in the 1890s village. About three hundred feet west of the Faribault cabin, visitors reach the 1857 Berger farm which features two horses and a garden. The two horses stay at the farm throughout the year, along with the tended garden and a beehive. These elements create an eerie sense that life continues on the farm, despite the fact that it is well over a hundred years old. From this farm the narrative of Minnesota settlement jumps to 1889 with a farm that reflects the change from subsistence to market farming. This farm has a bigger barn, a second out-building, and a larger home. The distance between the older and newer buildings gets shorter and shorter, echoing the escalating pace of settlement and socio-economic development.

Murphy's Inn, sandwiched between the farms and the village, blurs the distinction between the decaying but still-present past and the fully operational present. The inn is the only structure in The Landing that has a permanent guidepost complete with pictures of Major Murphy and the inn as it looked in the 1890s. Murphy's Inn spatially and materially links the trader's post and farm sites to the collection of nine homes, as well as to the general store, blacksmith, livery, priory, depot, lumber yard, town hall, gazebo, and church. The family homes and businesses are stocked with home goods authentic to the family and/or time period. Next to Murphy's Inn, for example, is the Wilkie home, dated 1880, which includes a bride's cupboard inscribed with the couple's initials and wedding date.[20] Just a few homes down and across the gravel road from Murphy's Inn is the Druke home, dated 1855, made of limestone and sand. And across the street is Civil War veteran John O'Connor's home, dated 1865–1880. The dates of the homes, from the 1850s to 1880s, blurs the central role that Indian agents, traders, and treaties played in the settlement of this land.

Through a curated representation of the Minnesota River Valley's past, The Landing grounds white agrarian settlement as the origin story of not only the land on which The Landing sits, but the broader space as well. While The Landing is open all year long, special events offer visitors an opportunity to interact with volunteer actors. The park's website invites visitors to "Visit *The Landing*—Minnesota River Heritage Park to discover how 19th-century Minnesotans established their lives on the frontier, farmstead and in villages. Historical buildings are laid out as a timeline from the pre-territorial era through the late 1800s."[21] The park offers summer camps such as "Wilderness Wit and Wisdom Camp" and "Little House on the River Camp," which the Three Rivers Park District's *2019 Summer Camps* brochure describes as follows: "[e]xperience log-cabin life in the Big Woods, just like Laura! Help with farm and garden chores, cook on a wood-burning stove, practice sewing, and attend school in a one-room schoolhouse. Play old-fashioned games and explore the outdoors. Take a trip to the General Store, where a note from Nellie Olesen awaits."[22] The Landing, like the popular book series and television program *Little House on the Prairie*, eschews the role that racism played in settler society.[23] In performing this decontextualized and anesthetized role of settler, visitors participate in a founding of the Minnesota River Valley in which the near absence of Dakota is not only normalized but folded into the narrative of progress. This reflects the ways, as Byrd explains, "[Indians] are typically spectral, implied and felt, but remain as lamentable casualties of national progress who haunt the United States on the cusp of empire and are destined to disappear with the frontier itself."[24] While visitors to The Landing go back in time to the beginnings of the farm and later the market economy, they need only step outside the park to see the continuation of these market practices, evinced by the eight gigantic modern-day grain bins just off the parking lot.[25] While settler colonialism is rooted in the wider space via The Landing, its economic impacts are evident not only on contemporary agricultural economics, but also on Indigenous nations.

Within a few hundred feet of The Landing is a sign for Mystic Lake Casino, the popular casino located on the Mdewakanton (Dakota) reservation. Mystic Lake is one of the most successful Native American casinos in the United States, and the Mdewakanton tribe that operates it is one of the largest benefactors in the state and country.[26] At night, search lights, constantly rotating in and out of the shape of a teepee, can be seen from miles away. Dakota activist and scholar Waziyatawin explains how for some Indigenous folks casinos "were hailed as 'the new buffalo' because [they] provided a single source of revenue that could provide for all the basic needs of our people, just like the bison did for Plains Peoples prior to their near annihilation." Waziyatawin argues that this phrase "the new buffalo" "denies the connection to land and life inherent in not just hunting traditions, but any way of life in which people draw their sustenance directly from the land" and that "the systematic disconnection (and dispossession) of Indigenous Peoples from our homelands is the defining characteristic of colonizing."[27] Waziyatawin illustrates how settler colonialism does not just influence systems of the dominant society, it remakes Indigenous cultures as well. Historical means of tribal subsistence are replaced with contemporary and contentious reliance on gaming.

Read through Indigenous epistemologies of place, The Landing makes visible the ways in which the site needs to be continually resettled. Closer examination makes visible what Indigenous studies scholars Corey Snelgrove, Rita Dhamoon, and Jeffrey Corntassel explain as the "contingencies" of settler colonialism. The authors discuss how "settlers have to be made and power relations between and among settlers and Indigenous peoples have to be reproduced in order for settler colonialism to extend temporally and spatially."[28] Examining the space beyond the borders of The Landing reveals how settler colonialism is extended "temporally and spatially." As an interactive site, The Landing invites visitors to use the past as a way to read and navigate the present and future.

The Landing is a space in which the representation of settlement works to recreate settlement and, as part of that, the disappearing of Indigeneity. It is this constant presence and absence, though, that makes the precariousness of settler colonialism most evident. It is, as Indigenous studies scholars Kay Anderson and Mona Domosh explain, "the contradictions inherent in national identities forged from positioning the colonized as both them and us; and from national identities requiring an imagined past, place and people, and yet denying that place and people a presence." By including the references to Dakota, The Landing keeps them in the narrative of settlement, but only at arms' length. The more complex history, the events before, on, and after 1851, are absent. In this way, the site reflects what Anderson and Domosh explain as "both them and us" and "denying that people and place a presence."[29] The Dakota are of this place though only as they disappear. This tension is evident in the name change to the site.

Recognition of the complexity of the site is evident in its 2008 renaming from Murphy's Landing to The Landing. The river, the land, the woods, and the occasional wildlife all work to unsettle the governing narrative of the site. The director of The Landing, Jefferson Spilman, was quoted in the *Star Tribune*, explaining that the name:

> reflects a change in the way the village is being seen—and a step away from seeing white settlement as the defining element of our history. . . . "We realized that Major Murphy was one person, who only lived here for 20 years," [Spilman] said. "Native Americans had a village here before he did, and were here for thousands of years. After Murphy, many people lived here. We decided that the river was really the key. 'The Landing' offers a broader way of thinking about human history here. Murphy will remain part of our story, but not the official name."[30]

While the naming of the park reflects the variety of ways visitors might encounter the site, the material, performative, and discursive components mitigate this potential. Examining The Landing and *Scaffold* reveals Indigenous refusal and radical resurgence as well as the precarities and contingencies of settler colonialism.

Rejecting Terms of Recognition and Asserting Indigeneity

The rhetorical connections between The Landing and *Scaffold* are illustrated by the public statements of Walker director Olga Viso and artist Sam Durant, insofar as they lay bare the extent to which settler colonialism drove the creation and acquisition of *Scaffold.* This section examines those statements, as well as the response by local and international Indigenous activists and allies. I argue that the combination of signs, along with the physical presence of activists, asserted Dakota conception of time and relation to land. The rejection of *Scaffold* and the Walker's attempt to represent Dakota is an example of Indigenous refusal and radical resurgence.

Durant and Viso explain that they intended the piece to educate white people like themselves and believed the Dakota and Minnesota's Indigenous past to be absent in the contemporary Minnesota gestalt. Durant stated that he envisioned the piece as "a learning space for people like me, white people who have not suffered the effects of a white supremacist society and who may not consciously know that it exists."[31] In using Dakota genocide as the raw material to contemplate state-sponsored executions, Durant simultaneously replays and denies said genocide. This reflects what Anderson and Domosh explain as the ways in which "implications of national identities that are continuously being constructed through narratives of the conquest of Native populations, and the disavowal of that conquest."[32] In positioning "white people" as the subject or audience for his art, Durant positions Dakota as the object. Indigenous people are confined to these colonialist terms of recognition. The activists' response reflects Coulthard's argument that Indigenous peoples must reject the "asymmetrical and non-reciprocal forms of recognition either imposed on them or granted to them by the colonial state."[33] Viso explained, "[w]e recognize, however, that the siting of *Scaffold* in our state, on a site that is only a short distance from Mankato, raises unique concerns. We recognize the decision to exhibit this work might cause some to question the Walker's sensitivity to Native audiences and audiences in Minnesota more familiar with this dark history."[34] Viso's statement invokes the stereotype of the stoic Native American relegated to the prairie. By pointing out that the work might be of particular significance to "Native audiences in Minnesota more familiar with this dark history," Viso makes clear the premise in operation which is that those familiar with this history are the exception and not the rule. Despite this objectification, activists on the site and in the press used *Scaffold* as a way to talk back to mainstream Minnesota.

On the website *Indian Country Today*, Konnie LeMay challenges the public apology of Viso and Durant. LeMay writes, "Intentionally or not, the idea that this horrific history of the Dakota people, embodied in a re-creation of the infamous mass gallows originally erected a mere 80 miles to the south, would stand in the area along with a giant spoon holding a cherry, an oversized rooster and mini-golf course rubbed salt into a 155-year-old wound."[35] LeMay decries not only Dakota genocide being relegated to a floating signifier but that it would be so "a mere 80 miles" from the site of the actual "infamous mass gallows." LeMay's comments reject settler colonialist time and place and assert Indigenous place and time. First, by naming "a mere 80 miles," LeMay calls out and rejects the colonialist demarcations of place and time. This comment works to assert that the significance of each space and as they are interconnected. Second, by depicting the harm caused by the sculpture as "rub[bing] salt into a 155-year-old wound," LeMay again calls out and rejects settler colonialist time. The wound remains; the harm caused by the Walker is interconnected with that of 1862. This reflects Audra Simpson's explanation of "settler time." Simpson explains, "[s]ettler time is revealed as the fiction of presumed neutrality of time itself, demonstrating the dominance of the present by some over others, and the unequal power to define what matters, who matters, what pasts are alive and when they die."[36] The assertion that this place is Dakota and to insist on visibility at the site of *Scaffold* pushes back on the invisibility of Dakota at both the site of *Scaffold* and The Landing.

The activists produced an alternative framing not only of the events of 1862, but also of the contemporary moment through seizing and reworking the terms of visibility. On the fence were numerous black-and-white posters with bold black lettering that read "Take it Down" along with the graphic of four black nooses. Underneath the large text on each sign were phrases including: "Shame on Walker," "Genocide is not Art," and "Never Forget 38+2." The mass-produced smaller signage directing the Walker to take the piece down was flanked by three handwritten bedsheets upon which "Remember their Names" and each of the names of the 38+2 were written. These large signs, alongside the mass-produced printed signs, transformed the 38+2 from being silent, inanimate objects to speaking, animate subjects. In the insistence on naming the 38+2, the activists pushed back on what Coulthard explains as "the subjectifying gaze and assimilative lure of colonial recognition."[37] By naming the 38+2, the activists made the Dakota the signifying agent and not *Scaffold* or the state. This rejection of the state as guiding the narrative, and assertion of Dakota place and time, was evident throughout the site. One of the hand-lettered signs, "The Great Sioux Uprising," invoked the institutionalization of the settler perspective of 1862 and inverted it to reflect Dakota perspective.[38] This is a particularly complex reading. Read through colonialist notions of time, the invocation of 1862 denotes the U.S.-Dakota war of that year and connotes the trauma and loss of particularly white settlers. Reading this through Indigenous time, the denotative and connotative meanings of 1862 are equally present in this moment. Through the lens of Indigenous time, this moment holds the same trauma and loss as well as resilience and survival. Contrary to settler colonialist renderings of the past, read through Indigenous logics, this argument resists foreclosure. This moment and this space are not folded into a specific date or a framing of that history, but rather assert Dakota existence. It is no longer a space or moment of genocide but, via the rejection of a specific time as well as interpretation of that time, one of genesis. Another hand-lettered sign, "Our Blood is not your Paint," which appeared to be written by a child, asserted interminable and intergenerational agency. This sign rejects the representation of Dakota as death and doom and instead asserts one of life and hope.

The activism at the site of the structure made visible echoes how Simpson explains the implications of Indigenous assertions of existence. She writes about the Kahnawà:ke, "[t]heir political consciousness and actions upend the perception that colonization, elimination, and settlement are situations of the past. Kahnawà:ke are not settled; they are not done; they are not gone. They have not let go of their themselves or their traditions, and they subvert this requirement at every turn with their actions." One of the key aspects of Indigenous refusal is a rejection of linear time or the separation of the past from the present. By being present on the site in person and through the multitude of voices represented in the handmade signs, the activists made their presence known. Through their rapid, collective, and consistent response to the structure, activists called out the Walker and as Simpson writes, "upend[ed] the perception that colonization, elimination, and settlement are situations of the past."[39] The activists called out the ways that Indigenous peoples are represented in public argument such as art. Reduced to the moment and act of genocide, Indigenous peoples are silenced. The activists seized on this opportunity and instead filled this attempt at silencing them with a cacophony of voices.

The immediate on-site protest was accompanied by sustained resistance amongst the Indigenous art community. Just days after the controversy broke, on May 29, 2017, All My Relations Arts, a Minneapolis Indigenous art gallery, issued a "Dakota Elders Announcement." Among the objectives of the meeting was to "identif[y] the twelve elders who are available and willing to attend the first face-to-face meeting with the Walker Art Center and Minneapolis Park and Recreation Board, Minneapolis administrator and the sculptor on Wednesday, May 31."[40] On May 30, the Walker hosted a press conference at which Lower Sioux Tribal Historic Preservation Officer Cheyanne St. John issued a statement. That day the Walker commissioned a company to tear down the piece and artist Sam Durant assigned the full copyright to the Dakota. After elders objected to the proposal to burn the pieces as a matter of Dakota spirituality and respectful use of the wood, the material was turned over to a tribal elder to be buried at an unspecified location.[41] It is important to consider the role that the activism on the site played in relation to that within the Walker and other channels.

Through their activism at the site, activists turned the space into a practice and amplification of being Dakota and Indigenous. Writing about recognition, Betasamosake Simpson explains how recognizing Nishnaabeg within others is a "process of seeing another being's core essence; it is a series of relationships. It is reciprocal, continual, way of generating society. It amplifies Nishnaabewin—all of the practices and intelligence that make us Nishnaabeg."[42] In all the ways that the activists made the space into one of Indigenous voices and resilience, it reflected the "generating [of] society" and the "practices and intelligence" that make the Dakota community. Hung on the back of the tent facing one of two roads leading to the sculpture garden and Walker parking lot was a massive white sheet with American Indian leader John Trudell's words "Intelligence is the antibiotic" painted on it. Trudell's oft-quoted directive, "intelligence is the antibiotic," made explicit the "practices and intelligences" that Betasamosake Simpson writes about and the activists made visible.[43] The large sign, the numerous other printed and hand-painted signs that covered the chain-link fence, and the activists on site, in the press, and at the table negotiating with the Walker, all demonstrated this intelligence. Further, through their continual engagement with the public, the Walker, the press, and other outlets, the activists invited others to learn. The fact that this specific phrase was the most pronounced—in terms of size of the sign, the writing on it, as well as its placement—all convey the idea that the "antibiotic" of "intelligence" was being offered to everyone. Surely there was a harm to the Dakota, to Indigenous in this misrecognition. This sign, though, invited everyone to recognize this harm and not only its effects on Indigenous peoples but everyone. Equally, it invited everyone to consider the healing that insisting on Indigenous terms of recognition could offer for everyone.

Reimagining Place through Indigenous Land Relations

The refusal to submit to the terms of visibility offered by the Walker via *Scaffold* reflects the generative potential of refusal. The activists' space became one of reasserting Dakota epistemologies. It reflected what Betasamosake Simpson, in her summary of Coulthard's work, explains as "a radical alternative to the structural and psycho-affective facets of colonial dominion." Betasamosake Simpson argues that these "inherent theories of resurgence are transformative and revolutionary. They are meant to propel and maintain social, cultural and political transformative movement through the worst forms of political genocide."[44] Refusal as generative and as a political move to assert Indigenous being and belonging was evident throughout the activism. Dakota activists remained at the site of *Scaffold* until it was taken down.

One last example from the Walker site demonstrates the power of Indigenous refusal and it remains with me, more so than any of the many other signs and conversations at the site. When I visited the site, two young men were stationed under the small tent with chairs and bottles of water. The men spoke with folks and answered questions. As I stood there taking it all in, a man and woman who had come from the Walker Art Center, as evidenced by the metal "W" pins on their shirts, approached the men. In a sort of indignant tone, the woman asked the men, "Don't you know art is supposed to provoke?" One of the men gestured to the other and said, "His grandfather is one of the 38." The woman persisted in her argument for a few moments until another woman standing nearby attempted to intervene and dissuade the first woman from pressing her argument. This intervention failed and the men and the Walker visitors dropped their discussion. As painful as this moment was, it is another example of the ways the activists resisted and insisted that they not only speak for themselves, but assert Indigeneity through the articulation of family and genealogical relations. Indigenous meanings of "grandfather" are not bound by legal relations or chronological, genealogical ordering. In that moment of speaking of and for their grandfathers, these men asserted Dakota familial relations. The words and actions of the men were striking for another reason as well.

In order for the young men to offer to engage in conversation with visitors, they had to literally face it. They had to look at the nearly complete, to-scale replica, and answer any range of educated to all-out harassing questions for days. They did not position themselves between the onlookers and the structure, instead they stood back across the sidewalk and near or under the three-sided tent. In order to engage the men in conversation, visitors had to turn their backs to the sculpture to face them. Indigenous refusal and recognition was evident in this invitation to move one's gaze away from *Scaffold* and the Walker's representation of the Dakota to the voices of Dakota themselves.

The tent, the signs, and the continued presence at the site by Dakota in which they demanded to be both subject and object all reflected a demand for recognition. The men insisted that their knowledge of the 38+2, of their community, be asserted in that space. In sharing that his grandfather was one of the 38, that man made the past visible and accessible in the present as well as the idea that the past is the present. Asserting Dakota being in that place did not elide or alleviate the harms, but it made visible the ways in which the present holds horizons of possibility. As Simpson explains in her analysis of the Mohawks of Kahnawà:ke, these Dakota men retained and enacted Dakota knowledge. In doing so, the men made Dakota epistemologies evident and through them a way of relating to place and each other outside of settler colonialist logics.

This refusal was generative in ways that worked within and thereby implicitly affirmed the guiding epistemologies of the Walker. In March of 2018, the Walker hosted a panel featuring four Native American artists who discussed "valuing the voices of indigenous artists."[45] In January 2019, the Walker announced an Indigenous public art commission that began with the words "Taku wanji unkoniciyakapi uncinpi. We want to tell you something," and ended with "Pidaunyayapi. We accept your offerings with thanks." The call explained that the Indigenous Public Art Selection Committee was composed of "Native curators, knowledge keepers, artists, and arts professionals, including individuals of Dakota descent and enrollment."[46] Finally, on September 17, 2019, the Walker announced the selection of artist Angela Two Stars (Dakota, Sisseton Wahpeton) as the finalist. According to the Walker, Two Stars:

> has conceived of a sculpture that is simultaneously a sculptural form, a gathering space, and an interactive work that provides a site for a broad audience to engage with Dakota language. Two Stars plans to incorporate text as well as a range of medicinal plants native to Minnesota, which represent a healing reconnection with Dakota language, culture, and traditional teachings.[47]

Okciyapi, which means "help each other" in Dakota, was unveiled in 2021. The piece is a round sculpture with a three-foot bubbling water pool in the center surrounding by stone concentric pieces inscribed with Dakota and Lakota words. Along with the babbling water are the recorded "voices of treasured elders sharing traditional stories, remembrances, anecdotes, and insights."[48] Okicapi, according to Two Stars, is central to the piece as the way that water and sound ripples as a metaphor for the legacy of figures like her grandfather, Orsen Bernard, and others whose legacy ripples across generations.[49] The stone pieces are chair-height and invite sitting or, perhaps more so, climbing and playing on that children might do. Two Stars's sculpture makes Dakota place relations accessible to all.

Efforts to construct the Shakopee Riverfront Cultural Trail (SRCT), an interpretive hiking trail along the Minnesota River and through The Landing took shape in May 2021. The Scott County Cultural Consortium (SCCC), which is made up of city of Shakopee, Scott County, the Scott County Historical Society, Three Rivers Park District, and the Shakopee Mdewakanton Sioux Community, has secured ninety-six million dollars for the first phase of the project. The 2.5-mile trail will include educational and experiential materials and run through downtown Shakopee and through The Landing. A historical research firm and architectural firm released the "Visitors' Experience Plan" which explains the five "themes" for the site: "The River Made This Place, Dakota Makoce: A Dakota Place, Canku Ota: Many Paths, River Resources, [and] Restoration and Renewal."[50] The goal of SRCT, according to the SCCC, is to "bring people together to (re)discover the Minnesota River's historical, cultural, and ecological significance, in order to build cross-cultural understanding among those who live in and visit the Shakopee area. The SRCT will become an iconic regional destination that demonstrates the value of incorporating place-based history and cultural heritage into local planning and development."[51]

According to the Shakopee Mdewakanton Community Facebook page, tribal chairperson Keith Anderson stated, "[w]e are excited to collaborate with the Shakopee, MN City Government, Scott County MN—Government, Three Rivers Park District and the Scott County Historical Society to develop a culturally significant trail along the Minnesota River in Shakopee."[52] Some of the principles of the project, laid out in the "Visitors' Experience Plan," are:

- DAKOTA VOICES AND VALUES should resonate through the experience, in both content and design. Interpretation should incorporate Dakota language and represent the resilience of Dakota people today.
- Much of the land along the SRCT is SACRED GROUND for today's Mdewakanton Dakota people, whose ancestors lived along the river in Tiŋta Otuŋwe. The trail's route passes through or near several cemeteries, sacred springs, and areas of archaeological, cultural, and spiritual significance.
- The experience should foster RESPECT; certainly, respect for Dakota burial mounds and the ancestors who are honored there; also respect for all those whose history is tied to the riverfront. The SRCT experience also will foster respect for one another and respect for the river, trees, plants, birds, and animals.

According to study, the trail will include nine "experiential zones." Dakota are woven throughout the zones, such an "EXPRESSING," which is focused on art, and "CULTIVATING," which is focused on Dakota food and agrarian development. The second to last zone is the "REFLECTING" which the Visitor's Experience Plan (VEP) explains as "Honors Dakota people's long and abiding relationship to this place and encourages respect for the ancestors who rest here as well as stewardship of the natural world."[53] This area in the trail park is in what is identified as "probably cemetery area." The zone immediately after this is "EXPLORING," which is described as "Engages visitors with the tangible past and helps them connect the themes and stories encountered along the trail." The VEP also identifies "zone moods" with the "REFLECTING" zone being identified as blue, or "contemplative, thought-provoking, restful, healing" and the "EXPLORING" zone being identified as purple, or "multi-layered, interactive, intriguing, content-rich." With the opening of the walk some way off, pending additional funding, there are many questions left to explore.

This new development at The Landing makes clear how recognition of Dakota, particularly at the sites of significance such as burial sites, remains caught between recognition and refusal. The development at Three Rivers Park makes visible the "recognition and refusal" insofar as Indigenous grounded normativity is made more evident and accessible. Representation of Dakota relationship with this place makes the precarity of The Landing and settler colonialism it reflects it even more evident. The themes of resonance, resilience, and respect attempt to mediate the tensions between Dakota and settler land relations. The principles of the project reflect an acknowledgement of the many relations that folks have with this place.

There are many strategies and nuances of Indigenous refusal of recognition as radical resurgence. While the activism at the Walker was a clear and arguably successful assertion of Indigenous refusal and recognition, the effects of the activism on the institution writ large are an ongoing question. Is there a productive space to be found in working within institutions founded and arguably still governed by settler colonialist epistemologies? The panel of Indigenous artists and Two Stars's work would indicate that there is. SRCT reflects a sustained effort to prioritize Indigenous land relations and voices. This project offers a way of thinking about the complexities of Indigenous representation when multiple agencies and institutions are involved. The next chapter will take up these same questions by examining how an Indigenous-led land reclamation project asserts Indigenous land relations as a way to expose and convert settler farmer nostalgia into support for Indigenous land relations.

CHAPTER TWO

Reparative Justice and Interventions in Settler Nostalgia

My ancestors came to Minnesota for two reasons—the offer of "free land" through the Homestead Act, and the freedom to practice their culture and religion. I am seeking to honor my ancestors and their/my culture and religion. This means doing right by the Dakota people who were forcefully removed to make the land available to settlers.

—John Stoesz, letter written in support of "State Building Code and Fire Code members of recognized tribes waiver process establishment" (H.S. 1042, S.F. 1087, 2021)

John Stoesz is a settler ally working for reparative justice for Dakota in Minnesota. Stoesz, former executive director of the Mennonite Central Committee Central States and 1973 graduate of southwestern Minnesota town Mountain Lake, spent the summer of 2014 biking around central southern Minnesota talking about land justice. Interviewed by the *Blooming Prairie Leader*, Stoesz explained, "[a]fter the [U.S.-Dakota] war, Dakota [N]atives were forcibly removed or killed—even in Minnesota. Those who weren't killed from disease, war or starvation were exiled, and many of us continue to benefit from the land that was settled by our European ancestors. I think it's past time for us to share the benefit with (the Dakota people)."[1] Recently retired and having given consideration to estate planning, Stoesz and his wife had sold their southwestern fifth-generation Minnesota farm and gave half of their proceeds of the sale to Makoce Ikikcupi (Land Recovery) project, a reparative justice project located in Granite Falls which focuses on restoring Dakota land and culture. Interviewed by the *Mankato Free Press*, Stoesz explained that "there should be a sharing of the land."[2] In their appeals for reparative justice, both

Makoce Ikikcupi founder Waziyatawin and Stoesz speak to the centrality of land to living a life that reflects one's culture as well as the role that land plays in restoring Dakota culture.

The "project for reparative justice" solicits financial support from settler descendants in order to create a space where Dakota people and culture may return and renew. According to its website, Makoce Ikikcupi "seeks to bring some of our relatives home, re-establish our spiritual and physical relationship with our homeland, and ensure the ongoing existence of our People."[3] This reflects what Indigenous studies scholar Leanne Betasamosake Simpson writes about as part of the importance of land-based knowledge and practices. She states, "[i]t is an embedded and interwoven spiritual, emotional, and social system of intelligence that fosters independence, community, and self-determination."[4] Interviewed by the *Free Press*, Waziyatawin explained her hopes for the land recovery project. "Our hope is that Dakota people who are now landless or who live in exile may come back to Dakota homeland and help establish communities committed to renewing our relationship with the land and strengthening Dakota ways of being. It's a long-term vision for Dakota land recovery."[5] The centrality of reestablishing Indigenous relations with land to the survival of Indigenous peoples and communities is articulated by Betasamosake Simpson. She writes, "[b]uilding diverse, nation-culture-based resurgences means re-investing in our own ways of being: regenerating our political and intellectual traditions; articulating and living our legal systems; language learning; ceremonial and spiritual pursuits; creating and using our artistic and performance-based traditions."[6] Makoce Ikikcupi is a project focused on Dakota political and spiritual culture as a way to bring exiled Dakota back to their community. This chapter explores the role of land and culture as it is evident in Makoce Ikikcupi appeals to settler descendants and in local newspaper coverage of the state of Minnesota Century Farm Recognition Program. Farms that are owned and operated by the same family for over a century have long been celebrated in Minnesota.

The most prestigious and visible recognition program is the Century Farm Program, sponsored by the Minnesota State Fair and Farmer's Bureau. The 2023 application explains what constitutes a century farm. The farm must be fifty or more acres and exist entirely within the state of Minnesota. The age of the farm must be verifiable "according to abstract of title, land patent, original deed, county land records, court file in registration proceedings or other authentic land records." A "family farm" is one that has been owned continuously, though not necessarily occupied, by a member of the family for one hundred years. "Family" is defined as "parents, grandparents, aunts, uncles, brothers, sisters, sons, daughters, first cousins and direct in-laws (father, mother, brother, sister, daughter, son-in-law)."[7] According to the 2021 Minnesota Century Farm Recognition Program application instructions, recipients receive a certificate signed by the governor, the president of Minnesota Farm Bureau, and the president of the board of the Minnesota State Fair.[8] According to the *Winona Post*, 2020 recipients also received "an outdoor sign signifying Sesquicentennial Farm recognition."[9] According to the *Minnesota Star Tribune*, the award is usually given at the family's local county fair.[10]

The program's establishment in 1976 was celebrated as part of the bicentennial "fair of a lifetime." Foundation director of the Farm Bureau, Ruth Meirick, explained in a 2019 *Star Tribune* article, "the Century Farm program began in 1976 piggybacking on the national bicentennial celebration to recognize families that persist through the trials and tribulations of farming. Many times, the applications are filed by the children of farmers, who are generally humble."[11] Agriculture was the original and remains a large focus of the fair. The first Minnesota State Fair was held in 1855, a year after the Minnesota Territorial Agricultural Society was founded and the state became a territory.[12]

Writing in 1976, bicentennial coordinator for the state fair, Karen Humphrey, explained why the state fair was the best venue for the Farm Recognition program. Humphrey writes:

> The purpose of the program was not a publicity gimmick or a "thing" to do for the Bicentennial, but an honest effort to discover just how many descendants still farm the same land as their pioneer ancestors did.
>
> The Minnesota State Fair is a likely place to undertake such a program. The State Fair, or more appropriately, the Minnesota State Agricultural Society, was organized in 1854 as the Territorial Agricultural Society. Ever since then, it has carried the theme "A Showcase of Minnesota Progress." Farmers, homemakers and manufacturers have brought their best to the fair not only to compete for prizes but to provide the impetus for others to make a better effort whether it be in growing corn, raising livestock, baking bread or building safer farm equipment.

I quote Humphrey at length to highlight a few specifics. First, Humphrey grounds the significance of the family farm in having "descendants still farm the same land as their pioneer ancestors did." This emphasis on "pioneer ancestors" privileges the settlement and continued inhabitance on a specific piece of land. Second, the Centennial Farm Recognition Program's establishment in the year of the country's bicentennial ties recognition of the duration and progress of the family farm to that of the country. The values, as Humphrey writes, having "brought their best" and "provid[ing] the impetus for others to make a better effort" are framed as that which is required to ensure not only the progress of the state, but of the nation. Examining discourses about settler farmer land relations and Dakota Indigenous land relations reveals the relationship between land and belonging.

I contend that these arguments about land intersect insofar as both settler colonialism and Indigeneity are most concerned with land and the precarity of that relationship. Close examination of these two intersecting arguments about land reveals two different relationships with it. For the Dakota, the Makoce Ikikcupi project is about creating a Dakota-centric space as a means to return from exile forced by the state of Minnesota and the United States, while the centennial and sesquicentennial farmers ability to settle land was the result of territorial, state, and national land laws. This analysis reflects what Indigenous studies scholar Noelani Goodyear-Ka'ōpua argues should be the focus; "land-centered literacies," as she writes, are "based on an intimate connection with and knowledge of the land."[13] This deep dive into the discursive rhetoric about land reveals the contrasting meanings between Indigenous and settler land relations. Indigenous studies scholars Eve Tuck and K. Wayne Yang state, "[w]ithin settler colonialism, the most important concern is land/water/air/subterranean earth (land, for shorthand, in this article). Land is what is most valuable, contested, required."[14] Indigenous land relations rely on the land as existence. Further, as the Makoce Ikikcupi project explains, the land recovery project is the way in which exiled Dakota relatives can return home. While settler colonialist land relations convey a deep appreciation for the land and the way in which it anchors socio-economic survival and belonging, that land relationship exists largely in memory and not as a lived practice. Examining the appeals to settler descendants reveals how appeals by activists like Stoesz, Waziyatawin, and others rely on the shared understanding of land as home and in particular the importance of existing on land as Dakota and thereby practicing Dakota culture.

This chapter analyzes the Makoce Ikikcupi land recovery project as it appeals to settler land logics and marshals them into arguments in support of Indigenous land relations. Waziyatawin, Stoesz, and other Makoce Ikikcupi activists articulate not only the significance of land return to Dakota culture, but how the act of supporting land return is a gesture of recognizing and seeking to amend the banishment of Dakota from the state. I begin with a discussion on why land as the central analytic helps get at the points of clash between Indigenous and settler colonialism. I also argue that this makes visible the terms by which settler colonialist relations to land are constituted and, more importantly, circumscribed. I then examine a collection of newspaper articles covering Minnesota Farm Bureau sesquicentennial and centennial award–winning family farms from 2000 to 2020. These newspapers' readership includes the communities and surrounding areas of farm recognition program winners. Newspapers include the *Faribault Daily News*, *Owatonna Peoples Press*, *Janesville Argus*, *Kenyon Leader*, *LeSueur City News*, *Londsdale Area News Review*, *Waseca City News*, *St. Peter Herald*, and *Northfield News*. I analyze these local, small newspapers so as to capture how these farm families tell their stories to their own communities. As smaller newspapers of smaller communities, the story of receiving this recognition is often given ample space. Finally, many of these communities continue to rely on the agricultural and related industries. The stories of these families, therefore, is in many ways the story of the larger community. I analyze the newspaper coverage and identify three themes: the disappearance of Indigenous, the making of settler immigrants as original inhabitants, and the logics of possession as they form the terms of belonging. Next, I examine the Makoce Ikikcupi website and newspaper coverage of the project. After that I discuss the ways in which the discourses about Makoce Ikikcupi frame the project and Dakota connection to land as enduring prior to and outside of the establishment of the state of Minnesota and that the return of land to the Dakota is a way to remedy exile. Finally, I close with reflections on how using Indigenous analytics of land can work to explicate settler colonialist terms of being and belonging.

Land as the Center

Centering land as the method and focus of analysis makes visible the way in which it constitutes identity. As communication studies scholar Molefi Kete Asante explains in a *Quarterly Journal of Speech* "#RhetoricSoWhite" discussion:

> [t]o dismantle Whiteness in rhetoric is to enunciate its characteristics, to denounce how it works but also to take Watt's point about "living in community" more seriously because it prompts us to consider voice and relationality to address the concealments of coloniality responsible for learning each other's histories and how they influence what we know about the world.[15]

The privileging of settler relations to land is an example of "concealments of coloniality" of which Asante speaks. Centering analysis on land and examining discourses about that relationship exposes this rhetoric that enables white privilege and undermine Indigenous agency. Closely examining Indigenous relations with land can work to make these and the ways they inform our understanding and relating to land and to each other visible. As activist and decolonialism scholar Harsha Wilia explains, "[d]ecolonization is a dramatic reimaging of relationships with land, people and the state. Much of this requires study. It requires conversation. It is a practice; it is an unlearning."[16] The "unlearning" of which Wilia speaks is evident in a willingness to critically examine taken-for-granted and even celebrated discourses about land and one's relationship with it.

While examining settler colonial logic risks perpetuating settler colonialism, I contend that centering land as an Indigenous analytic makes visible the components of settler colonialism as they intersect with and uphold dominant logics related to race, immigration, and land rights. As Indigenous studies scholars Corey Snelgrove, Rita Kaur Dhamoon, and Jeff Corntassel explain, "[w]hat good is it to analyze settler colonialism if that analysis does not shed light on sites of contradiction and weakness, the conditions for its reproduction, or the spaces and practices of resistance to it?"[17] This analysis of both settler colonialist discourses of the family farm and Indigenous discourses that intersect with these and assert Indigenous logics of land make visible the "reproduction" as well as the "spaces and practices of resistance." Additionally, this analysis explicates how these "reproductions" can be critically read so as to make visible the ways in which settler colonialism is self-circumscribing.

Land as analytic is part of a larger project in decolonialization as a study and praxis. Developing land as an analytic is part of the larger project, as Tiara Na'puti says, to develop "Indigeneity as analytic."[18] While Indigenous studies scholar Tiara Na'puti focuses on "discursive and communicative dimensions of Indigeneity as ancestry/kinship," I draw on scholars and activists and attempt to develop and apply land as analytic. Heeding Indigenous studies scholars Glen Coulthard and Leanne Betasamosake Simpson's call for "grounded normativity," I draw on Indigenous scholars and examine localized discourses about land both in rural farming communities and the Makoce Ikikcupi website and news coverage.[19] While I am mindful of how a focus on land risks further uptake of colonialist logics through "land-based preoccupations," I believe that a deep commitment to land as analytic can work can expose these logics.[20] Taking seriously the call to continue to develop "indigeneity as an analytic" and recognizing the role that this work can play in outing colonialist logics within our own field of study is part of the larger project of exposing and challenging power relations.

The interconnectedness and centrality of power, place, and person to Indigenous land logics cannot be understated. Indigenous studies scholar Vine Deloria Jr. and Daniel Wildcat explain the relationship between place and person:, "Power and place produce personality."[21] Betasamosake Simpson articulates the centrality of land to Indigenous "power" and how this conception of land differs from and challenges settler logics of land. She states:

> [t]he opposite of dispossession is not possession, it is deep, reciprocal, consensual attachment. Indigenous bodies don't relate to the land by possessing or owning it or having control over it. We relate to the land through connection—generative, affirmative, complex, overlapping, and nonlinear relationship. The reverse process of dispossession within Indigenous thought then is Nishnaabeg intelligence, Nishnaabewin. The opposite of dispossession within Indigenous thought is grounded normativity. This is our power.[22]

Indigenous conceptions of land and relations to and with it evade western conceptions which rely on possession, a relationship premised on separation and control. Framing relations with Indigenous land as "generative" invokes a living mutuality. As an "intelligence," "Nishnaabewin" is a way of being and being with as opposed to having and taking. Anticolonialism, according to Coulthard, is "a struggle not only for land in the material sense but also deeply informed by what the land as a complex system of reciprocal relations and obligations can teach us about living our lives in relation to one another and the natural world in nondominating and nonexploitative terms."[23] Coulthard illuminates how Indigenous logics of land rely on conceptualizations of land and relations with it as a system that exists outside of logics of land as material possession. Dakota conceptions of land are central to explicating what Indigenous studies scholar Noelani Goodyear-Ka'ōpua calls "land-centered literacies," which are "based on an intimate connection with and knowledge of the land."[24]

For Dakota, homeland, is central to being. In the first chapter of *Mni Sota Makoce: The Land of the Dakota*, authors Indigenous studies scholar Gwen Westerman and historian Bruce White explain the meaning of Mni Sota Makoce. They write:

> Mni Sota Makoce
> The land where the waters are so clear they reflect the clouds. This land is where our grandmothers' grandmothers' grandmothers played as children. Carried in our collective memories are stories of this place that reach beyond recorded history. Sixteen different verbs in the Dakota language describe returning home, coming home, or bringing something home. That is how important our homeland is in Dakota regardless of where our history has taken us. No matter how far we go, we journey back home through language and songs and in stories our grandparents told us to share with our children.[25]

Home exists as a place and it is held within Dakota and accessible via language shared between generations. In her dissertation, "Woyakapi Kin Ahdipi 'Bringing the Story Home': A History Within the Wakpa Ipaksan Dakota oyate," historian Katherine Beane explains:

> [w]e must return home to Minnesota, not just in a physical context (which is very necessary and important) but in an emotional one as well. We must assert our own right of belonging in these ancestral spaces of place, education, and being. This call for justice is rooted in our need to contribute back to our ancestral home of Mni Sota. As the original caretakers of the land, as storytellers, and as spiritual teachers to our children in our indigenous ways of knowing, all Dakota people carry the right to return home. Mitakuye Oyasin.[26]

As Beane explains, being home is central to "Indigenous ways of knowing." Western conceptions of land are based on a separation of one from land, from paternalistic stewardship to ownership, and therefore are incapable to reflecting Dakota land logics. Beane describes how being on Dakota land sustains physical and spiritual well-being. Learning and being Dakota is directly tied to being on Dakota land. Another element of understanding Dakota land logics is that they can never be, nor arguably should they, fully understood by non-Dakota. As Dakota activist Avery Jones explains in a recording on the Bda Maka Ska website, "some of those things are just for us."[27] Another aspect of land as an Indigenous analytic is that an analytic can never fully capture or convey the significance of that land. Reading and writing about Indigenous land relations is not the same as living them. This book, therefore, is a window into these analytics. There is a knowing with and of the land that can never be fully conveyed in any intellectual analytic. Settler colonialist land logics, though, are not constituted by a living and enduring relationship with the land.

Settlement Stories

Settler colonialism is evident in the newspaper coverage of Minnesota Farm Bureau sesquicentennial and centennial family farms in three themes. The first theme is the always-disappearing Indigenous or the folding of the removal of Indigenous into the narrative of settlement. The second theme is the indigenizing of the settler farmer, which works to fix immigration as a matter of acquiring and farming land, an economic and legal avenue that is largely foreclosed in the contemporary moment. The third and last theme is the possession and, in many cases, dispossession of land as a result of economic and governmental forces. Together, these themes reveal how Indigenous people are cast as ephemeral and settlers are recast as Indigenous, as well as how the terms of belonging are set and thereby circumscribed by the state. These themes reflect settler colonialism specifically as it intersects with the maintenance of agrarianism as part of citizenship and nation-building.

Disappearing Indigenous and Settler Claims to Land

The first theme is the ways in Indigenous peoples are felt but never fully present as an important part of settlement. Indigenous studies scholar Andrea Smith explains how Indigenous peoples "must always be disappearing in order to enable nonindigenous peoples' rightful claim to land. Through this logic of genocide, non-Native peoples then become the rightful inheritors of all that was [I]ndigenous—land, resources, [I]ndigenous spirituality, and culture."[28] The removal of Indigenous peoples is not noted or questioned in these narratives. As such, it is framed as inevitable and/or part of settling the frontier and nation building. The relationship between Indigenous peoples and original settlers is particularly pernicious. For example, one piece from the *Kenyon Leader* newspaper recounts the time of settlement in 1863. Terri Washburn writes, "[i]n those times, the area was still Indian territory, though Sands made friends with the [natives]. Still, when he was nominated for a seat in the State Legislature, he declined. It would have been too dangerous to leave his family alone and unprotected."[29] There are two important things to note in this passage. First, the characterization of "the area [as] still Indian territory" raises the question of whether the farm was established on unceded land. This question, though, is not raised. As a result, the matter of preemption, or basically, farming on reservation land and its implications for Indigenous peoples, is not raised. Second, the stereotype of Indigenous as dangerous is invoked by noting that even though "Sands made friends with the [natives]" he turned down a "nomination [in] the state legislature" because he thought it unwise to leave his "family alone and unprotected." Analyzing the story of Sands as a microcosm of the larger story of settlement reveals the idea that Indigenous peoples impeded not only familial success and security, but community and state.

The piece in the *Delano Eagle* newspaper also invokes the idea of Indigenous as savage and privileges settler perspective on the 1862 U.S.-Dakota war. Lisa Phillips writes, "Minnesota's statehood dates back to 1858—150 years ago. Back then people were dealing with Indian uprisings and staking their claims to open land."[30] This framing of settlement works to insulate the actions of state and federal government, such as their role in the "Indian uprisings" and the creation of "open land." This separation of the state seizure of land from Indigenous response to that seizure works to frame Indigenous actions as groundless. Instead of responding to the illegal taking of land and resources, Indigenous peoples are framed simply as perpetrators of arbitrary violence.[31] The indigenizing of settlers intersects with settler narratives of immigration.

This theme reflects the idea of Indigeneity being perceived, felt, but never fully present. This inverted logic reflects what Smith calls "the logic of genocide [which] holds that Indigenous peoples must disappear; in fact they must always be disappearing, in order to enable nonindigenous peoples' rightful claim to land."[32] The retelling of these stories works to normalize the removal of Indigenous peoples; their leaving is a necessary part of settler farmers arriving. Byrd writes about this as part of the frontier, Manifest Destiny, and nation building. She writes, "[Indians] are typically spectral, implied and felt, but remain as lamentable casualties of national progress who haunt the United States on the cusp of empire and are destined to disappear with the frontier itself."[33] Indigenous peoples are an important part of the settlement story, but only as subtext or the premise of settlement. As Indigenous studies scholars Kay Anderson and Mona Domosh argue in writing about the United States in contrast to European nations, "despite the formal recognition of Indian nations within the nation, and the enduring role of the 'native' in American notions of manifest destiny and the frontier, there are blind spots in public culture concerning colonial occupation of the indigenous lands of the 'Americas.'"[34] The retelling and circulation of Phillips's story, via the press, is reflective of the "blind spots in public culture" that Domosh and Anderson cite. Critically examining these discourses exposes and interrogates these otherwise "blind spots" particularly as they reflect and reinforce settler colonialism.

Indigenizing Settler Immigrants

The second theme is the way in which narratives of immigration work to indigenize settlers and their descendants. This narrative of indigenizing settlers also works to fix immigration to a specific historic moment as well as specific racial, ethnic, and nationalist genealogies. Immigration and settlement figure prominently in the stories of farm settlements. The White Bear Lake *Press* article, "Celebrating One Farm, One Family, 100 Years," begins with, "Per Olaf and Anna Johnson immigrated to America in 1883 from Sweden. In a story, that is hard to imagine in today's world, they sailed across the ocean to New York City."[35] By framing the experience of immigration as "hard to imagine in today's world," this piece affixes immigration to a specific experience and point in time. It narrows the story of immigration to oceanic crossings, Nordic immigrants, and heterosexual and nuclear families. Another piece explains how the grandfather of the current patriarch "immigrated from Tinnsja Lake, Norway to Capeman, Ill. in 1842," and that "[t]alk of fertile land in Minnesota brought him to Aspelund in 1859, where he homesteaded the original 120 acre farm."[36] While this piece reflects much of the same aspects of oceanic crossings of Nordic immigrants, it also omits the specificities of the passage between landing presumably on the east coast and the terms by which the promise of and means of "fertile land" was made.

Framing settler farmers as the original settlers works to depict them as Indigenous or original to the land. Tuck and Yang explain the distinction between immigrants and settlers: "[i]mmigrants are beholden to the Indigenous laws and epistemologies of the lands they migrate to. Settlers become the law, supplanting Indigenous land epistemologies. Therefore, settler nations are not immigrant nations."[37] Historically, the settler immigrant was framed as a superior, civilizing force against and over Indigenous ways of being. Today, and indeed many times throughout history, prominent discourses about immigrants and immigration flip this logic so that the immigrant is framed as inferior and a threat to settler civilization. It is the maintenance of these settler discourses of immigration that reinforce a specific and thereby foreclosed notion of immigrant. These discourses map immigration to a particular time frame and race, as well as to an outdated and largely economically unattainable agronomics.

Immigrant Nostalgia and Foreclosed Futures

The third theme in these discourses is the ways in which settler logics of land make evident the role of the state and market forces in setting the terms of belonging. The implications of the land as something to be possessed are evident too. Many narratives of the farm identify the role of domestic and global economics in undermining traditional farming and forcing families to move from subsistence to market farming. The subtitle "A Bygone Era," of the *Faribault News* article "Century Farms: Krause Family Land Honored as Century Farm," marks the economic changes to farming and their effect on the family farm. Ryan Anderson writes:

> Both David and Jean marvel at how much money is now involved in farming.
>
> When David started in the business, he could procure a bushel of corn for $7 or $8, he said. Now, that same bushel "goes for $350."

> When David and Jean visited the Steele County Free Fair this summer, they alighted upon a mammoth tractor with a $600,00 price tag, she recalled. "You need a lot of backing" to afford equipment that expensive—or "win the lottery."
>
> Farms now stretch hundreds upon hundreds of acres, David added. "Back in the 1940s, if you had anything over 80 acres, (people) laughed at you," because that was way more than enough "to raise a family on."[38]

Close examination of this passage reveals a few tensions. The first is between the money required to operate a farm decades ago and the amount needed now. The comparison of a bushel of corn going once for $7 or $8 and now $350, as well as the idea that the equipment needed for farming requires "win[ning] the lottery," is striking. These examples demonstrate the expanse between the economic context that drew in earlier farmers and that which they now face. This quote also grounds the origins of farming, not in things like total acreage, but in what is required "to raise a family on." This widening expanse between the current and earlier farm family's means of production results in fewer independent farmers.[39] The forces that set the context for the price of a bushel of corn, equipment, and what is required to raise a family are those of the state and industry.

In addition to market forces, cases of eminent domain laws being invoked to seize farmland make visible the role of the state in setting the terms of belonging. The Dorsey-Silker farm, featured in "Sesquicentennial Farm Carries on for Six Generations," lost land when "[i]n 1959, the U.S. Highway 14 project claimed 15 acres of the farm's northern land, including a spring-fed pond and several acres of the farm's best land."[40] The language and logic of "claiming" was evident earlier in claiming land to establish a farm. In this case, though, the logics and laws of claiming are still at work, though it is the state claiming land from farmers. Examining these discourses together makes the role of the state or government as ultimate arbiter of land evident. The "relationship of exclusion" which political science scholar Robert Nichols writes about is evident in that, whether as a result of market forces or eminent domain laws, the state sets the terms of belonging. Because they rely on the state to set the terms of land and belonging, and the state relies on logics of possession and dispossession, settler logics of land can never be relational.

Settler colonialism not only relies on state logics of place, but these logics are premised on possession and dispossession. In his analysis of the Chimney

Rock case, a Supreme Court case focused on Six Rivers National Forest and the use of a road by the U.S. Forest Service through land sacred to three Native American tribes, legal scholar Howard Vogel explicates the "power of the Anglo-American view of land as property, subject to title and possession, as an important feature of the American narrative embraced by most European Americans, against the meaning of land within Native American narratives."[41] A number of scholars have examined the relationship between settler colonialism and state and capitalist logics. Drawing on Deloria, Nichols develops the idea of "negative property rights." Nichols explains how "to claim property in something is, in effect, to construct a relationship with others, namely, a relationship of exclusion."[42] While Nichols focuses on the implications of this for Native American land claims, this insight is equally useful to understanding what Simpson refers to as a "settler precariousness."[43] Settler logics of land are recursive logics that at once create and are circumscribed by state and economic forces. As an assertion of Dakota land relations, Makoce Ikikcupi reveals, implicates, and inverts settler colonialism.

Makoce Ikikcupi and the Assertion of Indigenous Land Logics

Makoce Ikikcupi intersects with and exposes the economics of land dis/possession as well as provides a means beyond this by inviting settler descendants to contribute their own land holdings as a matter of reparative justice. Makoce Ikikcupi makes evident the ways in which, as Simpson explains, "Indigenous sovereignties and Indigenous political orders prevail within and apart from settler governance."[44] Makoce Ikikcupi demonstrates how Indigenous land logics can be supported through a critical read of settler colonialist land relations. It also makes evident how Indigenous land relations, in contrast to settler colonialist relations, do not rely on the state to set the terms of relating to land. The project reflects what Indigenous studies scholar Glen Coulthard explains as "resurgent politics of recognition." He writes that this type of work "is less orientated around attaining legal and political recognition by the state, and more about Indigenous peoples empowering themselves through cultural practices of individual and collective self-fashioning that to *prefigure* radical alternatives to the structural and subjective dimensions of colonial power.[45]

Makoce Ikikcupi is the epistemology and practice of Dakota land relations. Its mission is to create a space for Dakota lifeways. As such, land restoration through reparations is central to the project.

Land as Life

Makoce Ikikcupi focuses on land and what it means to Indigenous survivance and renewal.[46] The first page on the project's website, "Our Dream," explains why this land matters:

> As Dakota people, we consider Minisota Makoce (Land Where the Waters Reflect the Skies) to be our ancient homeland and we were the first humans to call this place home. Yet, in the last two centuries, Dakota people were systematically dispossessed of our homeland and we currently reside on about .01% (about one-hundredth of one percent) of our original land base within the borders of what is now the State of Minnesota. As a consequence, the vast majority of our people still live in exile.[47]

Not only does the project center their work on land as its home, but its dispossession and consequences are important as well. First, defining the land as "within the borders of what is now the State of Minnesota" makes it clear that the creation and continued existence of this place as Dakota is not dependent upon the state as a sanctioning or surveying agent. The relationship with land that Dakota have exists prior to and outside of the establishment of the state. Second, by describing the dispossession of the land by Dakota people in the past tense and then immediately describing the inhabitance of Dakota on this land in the present, the notions of time and place as linear are disrupted. This positions Dakota existence and presence outside of, and thereby extraneous to, timelines of colonization and settlement. While this passage centers Indigenous land relations, it also cites and indicts settler colonialist relations. By narrowing the scope of time to the "last two centuries" and using the language of "systemic disposes[sion]," quantifying the remaining Dakota land via the ".01%," as well as naming the agent of that dispossession as "the State of Minnesota," the site positions the state and state logics of land as the aggressor. This passage simultaneously asserts Dakota connection to this place as a prior to and outside of the logics of the state, and also makes clear that these logics were and remain a threat to Indigenous logics and existence.

The assertion of Indigenous logics of land is evident in the website's page "Our First Village," which explains how multiple villages within the site will "allow our people the opportunity to resume the ancient practice of traveling from place to place with the seasons and reclaim the foodways of our ancestors."[48] Food is culture. Reclaiming this place is a means, therefore, of reclaiming culture. Dakota relation to land and lifeways is evident in the inclusion not just of naming the "first village" but also in "traveling from place to place." The specific place(s) are not cited, making knowing of those places specific and exclusive to Dakota. The idea that Dakota have unique knowledge of the land is also amplified by the relationship between land, food, and culture. By framing the establishment of the village as a means of "allow[ing] our people the opportunity to resume the ancient practice," reflects the idea that the Dakota relationship with this land has not ceased, though it has been interrupted. Support of the villages therefore becomes a means through which Dakota take back up something they have always known, though, because of exile, been unable to practice. The urgency of reclaiming this relationship between Dakota land and people is clear.

Land and Reclaiming Relations

Living on Dakota land is central to ensuring the survival of Dakota people and culture. This reflects Coulthard's explanation of resurgent recognition. Makoce Ikikcupi's website explains, "The Makoce Ikikcupi project seeks to bring some of our relatives home, re-establish our spiritual and physical relationship with our homeland, and ensure the ongoing existence of our People. Our cultural survival depends on it."[49] "Spiritual," "physical," and "cultural," survival are all bound up in the re-establishment of lived relationship with this land. This passage also frames the "re-establish[ment]" of Dakota connection on the land as the means to "ensure the ongoing existence of [Dakota] People." As Betasamosake Simpson explains, "[w]e relate to the land through connection—generative, affirmative, complex, overlapping, and nonlinear relationship."[50] Restoring and strengthening the land is a continual, "generative" process, much like how story and ceremony are ways of doing culture. The "Our Dream" page states, "Our dream is to acquire lands within our ancestral territory where Dakota people may establish new communities based on sustainability and adherence to our ancient ways of being."[51] This reflects what Goodyear-Ka'ōpua explains as "land-centered literacies" in that Makoce Ikikcupi seeks to (re)establish culture that is derived from, relies upon, and is a relationship with the land.[52] Again, the relationship existed and continues to exist, as the reference to "ancient ways of being" indicates, though its fulfilment is dependent upon the "acquire[ment] land."

The land is not simply a means or an end, but that which makes Indigenous ways of being possible. In an interview with the *Free Press*, Waziyatawin explains what is at stake in restoration project. She states, "Our hope is that Dakota people who are now landless or who live in exile may come back to Dakota homeland and help establish communities committed to renewing our relationships with the land and strengthening our Dakota ways of being. It's a long-term vision for Dakota land recovery."[53] Note that Waziyatawin orientates the establishment of "communities" prior to "renewing relationships with the land and strengthening Dakota ways of being." "Ways of being" therefore depend on and exist only as a result of being on the land in community. While exile is evident in the context of state and federal laws, by not specifying which forms of exile, Waziyatawin opens "exile" to also mean simply being apart from Dakota land and thereby lifeways. This reflects what Coulthard explains as "what the land as a complex system of reciprocal relations and obligations can teach us about living our lives in relation to one another and the natural world in non-dominating and nonexploitative terms."[54] Land is a both a premise and realization of Indigenous survival, as opposed to settler colonialist land logics in which land is the means of survival. Waziyatawin also ties having a land to return to as the means of alleviating "living in exile." Makoce Ikikcupi is therefore not just a return of land, but a renewal of Dakota lifeways. Land and language are intimately connected as well.

Survival is not simply a matter of being on Dakota land, but land is tied to the sustainability of language and culture. The page "Our Dream" explains, "[i]f we do not implement a way of living in which our language is tied to our daily activities, our language will die and we will lose valuable survival knowledge."[55] Language emerges from Indigenous land relations. Indigenous writer and activist Diane Wilson explains the importance of the "Dakota way of living" to language.[56] Wilson recounts a conversation with Dakota elder Glenn Wasicuna at a Native American literature symposium who explained that "language is a person, a spirit." Wilson shares, "[w]hen people talk about how we've lost the language, they don't realize that what has really been lost is the Dakota way of living that invites the language to be present."[57] This reflects the beginning words of Westerman and White who explain the role of language in Dakota culture. They state, "we journey back home through language and songs and in stories our grandparents told us to share with our children."[58] "Language and song" are not part of the "journey back home," but rather are "the journey." They are at once the means and the ends. They reflect the ways that ceremony is the lived experience of culture. These discourses about Makoce Ikikcupi make visible Indigenous land relations and show that lived connection with land is central to being and sustaining Dakota lifeways. When Dakota and settler colonialist land logics are held up next to each other, the ways in which settler colonialism is a self-circumscribing logic are made clear.

Rejecting Land as Means and Asserting Land as Relations

In its appeals to settler farmer descendants, Makoce Ikikcupi holds up Indigenous land relations next to settler colonialist land relations, and in doing so, makes the distinction between them particularly visible. Makoce Ikikcupi is distinct because it works with the terms of recognition, but then in that space asserts the ways in which the state (the institutional and ontological authority by which the terms of recognition are set) has undermined Indigenous sovereignty. These discourses seize on settler farmer family history narratives and origin and the significance of family farms alongside illegalities and injustices of policies that made land "available" and marshals them into argument for reparative justice. Much like how settler logics of place require periodic suturing via signage, restructuring, etc. and need to shore up or rebuild or completely replicate, settler logics of place relations require retelling, reenactment, and signage. This makes visible how one's relationship to place or the terms of that relationship are economically and affectively constructed.

Stoesz centers his appeals on the role that land played in enabling his ancestors to practice their "culture and religion." The Makoce Ikikcupi project, as Waziyatawin explains, is about land as restoring Dakota culture and lifeways.

Land is the fulcrum for both Stoesz and Waziyatawin. There is an important distinction, though, between Stoesz's appeal and the ways that the centennial farm families frame the importance of the land. While Stoesz frames his family farm as a reprieve from exile and thereby the ability to practice his culture, the Farm Bureau families name but do not invoke being forced out of their countries of origin or the role that land plays in enabling them to practice their culture. While some identify the family farm as a place to preserve and practice one's native culture via such things as speaking Norwegian and eating lutefisk at Christmas, a particular piece of land was not required to do so.[59] Farmland itself, and not land specific to their culture, enabled family farmers to practice their ethnic and religious origins without threat of banishment. For Dakota communities, specific land is the culture and religion. Thinking about Makoce Ikikcupi, Stoesz's appeals, and the centennial farmers through this lens reveals how Stoesz is attempting to create a space for empathy and allyship. For Stoesz and other settler descendants, though, the state is the mediator of settler land relations. For Waziyatawin and Makoce Ikikcupi, Indigenous land relations exist outside of and against these institutions. This is why supporting Dakota land return requires not simply empathizing with the Dakota or offering one's own land, but rather offering financial resources and the land.

This rhetorical move reflects what Vogel argues must occur as part of the larger work of restorative justice in Minnesota. In his discussion, "Healing the Trauma of America's Past: Restorative Justice, Honest Patriotism, and the Legacy of Ethnic Cleansing," Vogel explains that in order for restorative justice to occur, "[i]t must embrace its transformative potential through *courageous remembrance of the truth of the past* as a first step in order to foster dialogic acts of hope that manifest respect in its deepest sense, including reparations, so that life may be lived beyond the burden of the past."[60] Makoce Ikikcupi's appeal to settler descendants is a sort of "dialogic act of hope" that Vogel writes about. These discourses are a way for settler descendants to acknowledge the past and actively participate in helping to restore Dakota land and Indigenous land-based logics.

By placing responsibility for Dakota placemaking on the shoulders of settlers, Makoce Ikikcupi reflects what historian Paulette Regan explains as "the collective responsibility we bear for the status quo."[61] After laying out the goals of the project, the homepage titled "Our Dream" cites the role of settlers. It states, "[t]hrough settler donations to this project, we have now purchased our first parcel of land in pursuit of this dream. . . . We appreciate your interest in Dakota land recovery. Wopida unkenic'iyapi! We give you thanks!"[62] In an interview with the *Mankato Free Press*, Waziyatawin places the responsibility for both historical wrongs and future opportunities to do right on the shoulders of settlers. She states, "The land recovery project is about trying to address those historical wrongs by working toward justice. . . . This project creates space for Minnesotans to personally contribute to our struggle for justice through an act of personal reparations."[63] The page "Our First Village" closes with a recognition of "all [of] our supporters who believe in the importance of reparative justice and the right of Dakota people to live within our traditional territory, nina wopida ecic'iyapi (I give you all many thanks)!"[64] The project bridges the past and the present by inviting settlers' descendants to not only acknowledge their complicities, but repair the harm by supporting Dakota land relations.

By grounding this analysis land, we are able to see and more fully understand Indigenous land logics and how they expose and critique settler colonialist land logics. What is striking about the Makoce Ikikcupi project is that it simultaneously deploys and interrogates settler logics of land and marshals this into appeals for financial support of Indigenous Dakota land logics. Both it and Stoesz invite potential supporters to consider their own relation to land as a juxtaposition to what specific land means to the Dakota. In doing so, it makes visible the potential and limitations of allyship.

CHAPTER THREE

Dakota Memory Maps and Re-Membering the Land

Introduction of traditional and sometimes sacred places erased in public community memory is important to the task of recognizing this region as Dakota homeland. This re-cognition is important for the healing of the Dakota people, of the non-native residents of the area and of Mnisota Makoce herself.

—"About This Site," Bdote Memory Map

The online Bdote Memory Map is a digital-humanities mapping project that explains the Dakota history and connection to sites of significance including and surrounding Bdote. Bdote is the confluence of the Minnesota and Mississippi rivers, the origin of the Dakota people. According to the site, seeing this and other places as Dakota is a type of "re-cognition" and part of the "the healing" of Dakota and non-Dakota people and of these places. The map is intended to be a doorway or a "glimpse" into seeing places through Dakota eyes. The site invites users to explore it as a preface to visiting and engaging with the actual places featured in it. The "About this Site" page explains that the map is "intended to be a glimpse, a beginning point, a way to imagine learning FROM Dakota people. Recognition of the connection of Dakota people to this place (these places) leads to hidden truth in viewing history and contemporary relationships."[1] The website makes visible and partly accessible Dakota ways of understanding and relating to these places.

The online Bdote Memory Map and its more recent offshoot, "Learning from Place: Bdote," first took public form as an art installation.[2] The Bdote tour is administrated by the Minnesota Humanities Center and is a guided tour of many of the sites on the map led by Dakota educators. The online Bdote Memory Map, according to the page "[a]bout this [s]ite," "began as part of the 'Urban Indian' installation on Franklin Avenue in Minneapolis in 2005."[3] The inclusion of the location of the installation on Franklin Avenue is noteworthy. This area is known as the American Indian Corridor; the American Indian Cultural Center, Little Earth Housing Complex, and many other Native American businesses and cultural resources are located here.[4] Also of importance is the fact that particularly since, but not beginning with, the Indian Relocation Act, Indigenous peoples have been pushed into urban settings like this area.[5] Noting the gallery and the inclusion of "urban" in the title highlights the experience of urban Indigenous peoples as a result of the Indian Urbanization Act and other government actions.

In 1993, Ancient Traders Gallery, now All My Relations Arts, featured Mona Smith's installation *Urban Indians*. The interactive piece featured two maps of the Twin Cities and a mock-up of a Minneapolis police car. One of the maps featured the Mississippi and Minnesota rivers as well as a few Dakota place names and historical photographs. This map included blank Post-it notes and invited participants to "add their own written memories and stories of traditional Dakota sites."[6] The other map, across the room, featured "detailed information of Dakota place names for areas that are now completely urbanized."[7] Also included in the installation was the back half of a car made to look like a Minneapolis police car. This piece was a reference to a 1993 incident in which two Minneapolis police officers, Marvin Schumer and Mike Lardy, placed two Indigenous men, Charles Lone Eagle and John Boney, into the trunk of their squad car.[8] Lone Eagle's leg was injured when the trunk door was closed on it and the ride to hospital, a short distance away, took an unreasonably long time.[9] Projected onto the car were video recordings of Indigenous people talking about how the 1993 case affected them. According to Minnesota Public Radio, Smith was "attempting to convert the trunk from a symbol of abuse to a place where voices are heard. Smith says Indians aren't listened to very often; you don't find them sharing stories on the TV. So she felt it was important to give a voice to people who are often unheard."[10] Smith's work countered the silencing of Lone Eagle and Boney as well as that of the greater Indigenous community.

Smith's art was a way in which Indigenous in Minnesota talked back to not only Minneapolis law enforcement, but the also the larger community.[11] The projection of living, speaking Indigenous peoples onto the shell of a Minneapolis police car worked to insist the gallery guests engage with this incident of police violence through Indigenous perspectives. The more animate audio and visual elements of the piece literally and figuratively spoke over those of the inanimate material elements, the Minneapolis Police Department (MPD). The timing of Smith's work was crucial. At the specific moment in which Indigenous voices were silenced, Smith instead inserted and asserted Indigenous voices. She visually and aurally laid Indigenous voices over those of the MPD. With the video installation situated between the two maps of Dakota places and stories, the gallery space became a tool to see, hear, and remember this and the broader Mississippi and Minnesota River spaces as Dakota. Using historical photographs along with contemporary handwritten notes of memories and stories, the space asserted the centrality of place over time. This all worked to jettison MPD both insofar as it serves as an arm of the state as well as is representative of the state's literal and epistemological authority. Smith's work reminded all of those present that the space is Dakota.

Smith's *Urban Indians* was the beginning of what is now the Bdote Memory Map, an interactive website that features series of images, videos, and other resources correlated with sites of great significance to the Dakota community.[12] The map, sponsored by the Minnesota Humanities Center and created by Allies Media, is a resource particularly for K–12 educators and students. According to Minnesota Humanities Center Vice President Matthew Brandt, as quoted by *Red Lake News*, "[f]or both American Indian students and their non-Indian classmates, the Bdote Memory Map place-based approach connects them to this place, to each other, and to themselves."[13] One of the sites on the Bdote Memory Map is Fort Snelling. This is where 1,600 Dakota children, women, and elderly were held over the winter of 1862–1863 before being exiled to the Crow Creek reservation.[14] Historic Fort Snelling is also one of the most notable sites in the state of Minnesota.[15] It is the site of Dakota genesis, and also a site of genocide.

Examining the Bdote Memory Map and Historic Fort Snelling reveals how Dakota land relations are negotiated and made visible through Indigenous-centered mediums such as the website, gallery installation, and tour. Dakota land relations are also made visible through largely settler colonialist institutions such as the Minnesota Historical Society (MNHS) and others which oversees Historic Fort Snelling at Bdote. Historical sites, such as Historic Fort Snelling and the twenty-five other historic sites the MNHS operates, therefore require a negotiation with Indigenous communities.[16] This process gets to the many questions of Indigenous representation, such as should Indigenous place relations even be shared with the non-Indigenous community? There are risks and harm to Indigenous communities when Indigenous place knowledge is shared.[17] Yet, Indigenous communities must articulate land relations in order to protect land. How, therefore, can Indigeneity be represented without being folded into or annulled via the dominant, operating logics of institutions such as MNHS and others? Similar to the Trudell signage at the Walker, the signage at Historic Fort Snelling reflects an offering of or invitation to consider Dakota land relations.

Indigenous refusal and resurgence is evident in the Bdote Memory Map and Historic Fort Snelling. The Bdote Memory Maps are a glimpse into Dakota grounded normativity and the role that these particular places play in it. The Bdote Memory Maps, with its focus on Dakota language, personal narrative, as well as imagery and art, assert Dakota relationship with this place. The maps not only work to re-member this place as Dakota, but to invite all participants to consider their relationships with the places that hold significance for them. As Historic Fort Snelling lies within Bdote, I also examine this site. I examine the signage, built and rebuilt structures, and pathways. Examining the site through Indigenous logics makes visible the ways in which Dakota relationship with this place is not—indeed, cannot be—contained within or made intelligible through settler colonialist logics. Close examination of the newer signage and built spaces reveals how Indigenous communities work within settler colonialist institutions like MNHS and negotiate terms of visibility to make Indigenous land relations visible. The tension between Bdote and Historic Fort Snelling has existed for centuries.

Historic Fort Snelling at Bdote

What is now named Historic Fort Snelling, as well as the original and much larger site of the area of the fort, was built in Bdote. "Historic Fort Snelling" is the name given to the site by MNHS, as a guide at the site when I visited in June of 2023 explained, to distinguish the site from the other nearby "Fort Snelling" places such as the Fort Snelling State Park, Fort Snelling National Cemetery, Fort Snelling Memorial Chapel, and others. In its original layout, Fort Snelling included much of what is now Fort Snelling State Park.[18] "Bdote," as Westerman and White explain, is the Dakota word for "confluence" and includes the meeting point of the Mississippi and Minnesota Rivers, as well as Mni Owe Sni (Coldwater Spring), Minigaga Wapka Cisstina (Minnehaha Falls), Wita Tonka (Pike Island), Kaposia (Saint Paul), Oheyawahi (Pilot Knob Hill), and other sites of importance.[19] Bdote, the confluence of the Minnesota and Mississippi rivers, the site where Historic Fort Snelling is located, is the site of Dakota origin. The significance of the site and how it should be managed has long been a point of contention between the state of Minnesota and Indigenous activists.

Historic Fort Snelling, Minnesota's first national historic landmark, has been a site of contention, particularly since 2008 when efforts to restore parts of the mostly rebuilt site were met with protest.[20] A wagon train intended to commemorate the 2008 state sesquicentennial made visible the tensions over how Historic Fort Snelling's role in state history should be remembered. The wagon train was followed by a group of Dakota activists who met at Indian Mounds Park in Saint Paul and marched to the capital where they stood across the street and held protest signs. The "Seven Council Fires" group representative Chris Mato Nunpa explained to MPR "[u]nless the history of Minnesota includes massive land theft, broken treaties and genocide, then it will still remain a whitewashed, literally a whitewashed history."[21] The group then walked in front of the wagon train and, as it entered Historic Fort Snelling, positioned themselves to meet the wagon train with signs reading "sesquicentennial: 150 years of lies" and "will you kill us again?"[22] The fort site remained open to visitors with only operating costs covered for the past few decades. Probably the most notable structures, the fort walls and the round tower, were rebuilt in the 1960s after construction was spurred on by the state centennial. Recent developments at the site have sparked new controversy.

The attempt by MNHS to acknowledge Dakota connection to this place started back in 2019 when a new sign which read "Historic Fort Snelling at Bdote" replaced the older sign which read "Historic Fort Snelling." Within weeks of the new signage appearing, a group of Republican state senators threatened to cut MNHS funding by 30 percent.[23] During this same time, the new sign was vandalized with the "at Bdote" colored over in marker so that it blended into the blue background of the sign. A short time after this, the sign was replaced with a new one that read "Historic Fort Snelling." The controversy over the sign and other elements of the site is representative of the continued tensions over how this place should be named and interpreted.[24]

The relationship of Dakota to the site, as well as that of Dred Scott and Japanese Americans who served at the fort during World War II, features more prominently in the updated visitor's center, web page, and programming. Through state allocations and private donations, MNHS renovated a former soldier's barracks into a newly opened visitor's center, added three outdoor installations, and developed new programming. The new website, updated April 2023, continues to reflect the tensions over the naming and meaning of this place. The site's homepage, "A New Vision for Historic Fort Snelling," explains, "[h]ere on Dakota homeland known as Bdote, come learn, share and connect to all of the complex stories of those who crossed paths here and shaped history in Minnesota—from the Dakota, Ojibwe, and enslaved people, to fur traders, immigrants, soldiers and veterans."[25] As the next section illustrates, though, Dakota land relations are not contained or conveyed within settler colonial logics of place or time.

Bdote Memory Map and Dakota Place Relations

Indigenous land relations are evident in the online Bdote maps. As Historic Fort Snelling is in Bdote, Indigenous land relations are evident there as well. Examining these virtual and material spaces reveals three interrelated themes. The first theme is the foregrounding of place and its significance irrespective of people, events, or built structures. The second theme is a rejection of settler colonialist time or the disturbance of the strict ordering of the past, present, and future. The third theme is that signage and built spaces indicate but do not demarcate Dakota place relations. Rather, these spaces and signage make evident the ways Dakota land relations refuse and resist settler colonialist terms of recognition and thereby are more fully visible.

Foregrounding of Place over Time

Bdote is the center and legend of the online map. What is first noticeable about the homepage is the rivers. Saint Paul and Minneapolis are included in the map, though there is no dot by the name and the shading of the labels is fainter than the other place names. Haha Wakpa, the Mississippi River, is labeled, though the font and text are shaded so that the blue water itself, along with the other rivers and lakes, are more noticeable than the written text. This makes correlating the exact location of these cities possible only by reference to Bdote as well as the bodies of water. The places on the map, indicated with a big red dot, include Mni Owe Sne (Coldwater Spring), Fort Snelling, Bdote, Owamni, Kaposia (Saint Paul), and Wita Tonka (Pike Island). Fort Snelling is the only location with a red dot that does not have a Dakota name. Conversely, Bdote is the only Dakota name on the map without an English name. As a result, Bdote and Fort Snelling are juxtaposed with each other; Bdote is a Dakota place and Fort Snelling is clearly not.

Bdote is not only the center of the online map, but the key to it. To navigate the map, users have to orientate themselves in reference to Bdote and not the nearby major cities of Minneapolis and Saint Paul. This map makes Bdote the signified and the signifier; the location and meaning of all other places can only be understood in relation to Bdote. This reflects Vine Deloria Jr.'s explanation of how many Indigenous nations have a "sacred center at a particular place." He writes:

> [t]his center enables the people to look out along the four dimensions and locate their lands, to relate to all historical events within the confines of this particular land, and to accept responsibility for it. Regardless of what subsequently happens to the people, the sacred lands remain as permanent fixtures in their cultural or religious understanding.[26]

The land and water are the focus of the Bdote map. Users navigate the map through correlating places via land formations and waterways. This is in sharp contrast to settler colonialist maps in which users correlate their place in relations to sites, street names, and structures. In the Bdote map, users must have knowledge of the land. The online map is populated with the land as well as a multitude of voices, sounds, and images. This conveys the idea that the land is not something to be understood in an abstract or quantitative sense, but in an experiential and relational sense.

The online Bdote site is enlivened with individuals, groups, and videos of significant places. Clicking on each of the red dots leads to a page which has a block of text on the left and a list of picture/video icons on the right. Some pages have four icons and others have as many as sixteen. The icons include contemporary video stills, black-and-white photographs and maps, and some audio clips. Clicking on Bdote takes the user to a page with an explanation of the term in a block on the left side along with a menu of brief videos on the right. The picture icons of the videos include outdoor audio-video segments, paintings and maps, and Dakota speakers. The first one is "Mato Nunpa, THE Bdote," the speaker explains that Bdote means where two waters meet, though this one, the confluence of the Minnesota and Mississippi, is particularly important. He shares that he heard stories from his mother and other storytellers who explained the Dakota Oyate and the "genesis" of the Dakota. In the next video labeled "Know Where you Are," Ethan Neerdaels talks about Bdote as the camera begins with a panoramic view out over the confluence. The camera then pans to Neerdaels talking to a group of schoolchildren outside. The visual imagery of water and outdoors contrasts with the previous video of Nunpa which was a close-up shot of him speaking. Neerdaels's video invites viewers to engage in the confluence of moving waters. All of the live elements are significant because they reflect how the site always has had, has, and will have the significance of which Neerdaels speaks. The imagery of the children learning in the space also works to blur the distinction between the past, present, and future.

Rejecting Settler Colonialist Time

The digital Bdote Memory Map makes Dakota past, present, and future equally and immediately accessible. While the dates of some material are evident in maps and photographs, the instant accessibility of it all makes it immediately present. Older photographs, within the context of Dakota speakers and videos of the places as they sound and appear now, are all encapsulated in the website. In this way, the distinction between the past and present is mute. As users navigate and interact with the content as they choose, they blur the distinction between the past, present, and future. This reflects what communication studies scholar Greg Dickinson, who draws on historian Doreen Massey, explains as "the experience of multiple stories so far, the layering of multiplicities and heterogeneities, and of the non-linearity of past/present/future."[27] In the context of the website, the distinction between past, present, and future is not only rendered mute, but the distinctions between them are made unintelligible and irrelevant. In understanding place, users navigate between and coalesce past, present, and future. All are the same; all are simultaneously present. In this way, Indigenous land relations are asserted outside of settler colonial impositions of time. Indigenous refusal and radical resurgence are evident in one of the new outdoor installations at Historic Fort Snelling.

A new installation, the second visitors encounter, articulates Dakota knowledge particularly as it asserts Dakota experience and resilience. I focus on Peter Lengkeek's post because it appears first of the three similar posts. It is foremost as visitors walk from the parking lot to the visitor's center and its focus is on Lengkeek who is both a member of and leader in the Dakota nation and a soldier in the U.S. military. The 38+2 Commemorative Ride, Dakota nationhood, and U.S. nationhood are framed under the title of "hope."[28] This is one of three bifold post signs that line much of the paved walkway between the visitor parking lot and Plank visitor center. The next post is titled "identity" and focuses on the experience of members of the Women's Army Auxiliary Corps and Chinese American military translators who were stationed at the fort during World War II.[29] The other post is titled "service" and includes pictures and snippets of the experience of Second Lieutenant Clifford Brunzell, who trained at Fort Snelling. Though the three posts are similar in design and aesthetics, the text and images are small so that they cannot be read simultaneously or from more than five or so feet away. Visitors must pause in front of each one to read all of the text and consume the images. The Lengkeek post is the only one of the three to highlight the present as evinced in its use of present tense verbs and color images.

The focus of the Lengkeek post is on reconciliation, healing, and hope. The top left side of the panel, across from the right panel that reads "hope," are the words "Bring races together and begin the healing." Between this quote and the next block of text is a picture of Peter Lengkeek in army fatigues. Beneath that picture it reads:

> Peter Lengkeek, citizen of the Hunkpati Dakota Oyate, has long been an advocate for his people, including remembering and honoring his own ancestor who was hanged in Mankato in 1862. He speaks of hope.
>
> These riders, they come from all over. Canada, Montana, Iowa, South Dakota, North Dakota, Minnesota. There's even a guy here from Austria.

Lengkeek is referring to the 38+2 commemorative ride that begins in Flandreau, South Dakota and ends on December 26 at Reconciliation Park, Mankato, the site of the 1862 execution.[30] The Dakota Commemorative Ride is an annual 330-mile horse ride from Flandreau, South Dakota to Reconciliation Park in Mankato, Minnesota that honors the 38+2. The final day of the ride is always December 26, the day of the execution of the 38+2. Instead of silent remembering, the culmination of the three-plus weeks' ride is the sound of horses and whoops; the sight of children, women, and men on horses; elders and supporters layered in lots of winter clothes with frozen breaths in the air circling around the horses. A sense of this is captured in the four images which are overhead: a group of riders coming into Mankato, Lengkeek and his horse and trailer, Lengkeek holding an eagle staff while he and Mary Herbst hug, and Lengkeek in his U.S. military fatigues. The image below the quote is of Lengkeek at one of the rides embracing Mary Herbst. The photo is captioned: "Peter Lengkeek and Mary Herbst at Mankato, December 26, 2009. Lengkeek's ancestor was hanged in Mankato in 1862. Herbst's ancestor was a U.S. Army soldier who stood guard during the hanging." The text box on the bottom of the picture reads:

> What we're trying to do here is we're trying to reconcile, unite. Make peace with everyone because that's what it means to be Dakota. To be Dakota means to walk in peace and harmony with every living thing. That is our way.

The other pictures and text are of the riders making their way into Reconciliation Park and of a rider and their horse. While the first image of Lengkeek in his fatigues invites identification with U.S. military service and/or nationalism—Dakota and U.S.—a strict interpretation of this as a representation of U.S. nationalism is complicated by the other image of Lengkeek and the Herbst embracing.

Lengkeek's explanation that "to reconcile, unite" and to "make peace with everyone" reflects his Dakota culture and echoes Vine Deloria Jr.'s argument of how culture is not only an "an intelligence system" but one that is derived from this particular place. In one way, Lengkeek's words are attached to the 38+2 ride and his other work with his tribal nation. In another way, Lengkeek's words are attached to and derived from this site, Historic Fort Snelling, as an icon of U.S. military history. This specific phrasing, though, rejects the U.S. military's authority to set the terms of recognition for Lengkeek and the Dakota nation. Lengkeek defines his role as a Dakota first and foremost. And, importantly, he does not reject his identity as a U.S. military soldier, but subsumes it under the larger identity and values of "hope and reconciliation."[31] The inclusion of Herbst, as a descendant and thereby stand-in for her U.S. military ancestor, ties hope and reconciliation to both Dakota and U.S. nationhood. Tying U.S. and Dakota nationalism together in "reconcili[ation] and "mak[ing] peace" become part of both national identities and values.

Lengkeek's dual identity as a Dakota and U.S. citizen and soldier makes visible the idea of competing sovereignties both for Dakota people and the site. Simpson explores the use of Haudenosaunee passports and the way in which they function as a refusal of state recognition and authority and an assertion of Indigenous recognition and authority. In her examination of the Mohawks of Kahnawà:ke, Simpson explains how "one does not negate the other, but they necessarily stand in terrific tension and pose serious jurisdictional and normative challenges to each other."[32] In highlighting Lengkeek as both a member of both the Dakota and U.S. nations, the "tension" as well as the "jurisdictional and normative challenges [these two identities pose] to each other" is made visible and accessible. This carries over to the site as well. Lengkeek becomes emblematic of the tensions between the site as central to Dakota and U.S. nation building. Visitors are thereby positioned in that literal and figurative space whereby they can productively negotiate those tensions themselves.

Just as the post at the entrance to the site productively plays with the placement and meaning of Bdote and the origin of Dakota, the reference to "here" and inviting "reconciliation" and "unit[ing]" opens the meaning of the site up to not just past history, but present and future reconciliation. The post also invites readers to consider the U.S.-Dakota war through Dakota eyes and, like many U.S. wars, to see it as a matter of defending one's nation. Titling this post "hope" further undermines a strictly past-looking interpretation of the site. *Hope* is a verb. It is an action in which the present hails, invites, or bridges the present with the future. Framing what they are "trying to do here" in the present tense, as "reconcile" and "unite," invites visitors to see the site not for what it means historically, but for what it also means in the present and can mean in the future. This is an assertion of Indigeneity and what it means to be, in this case, Dakota. The significance of telling Lengkeek's story at this place, framed as an icon of state and nation building, works to assert Dakota belonging and disturb both the timeline of U.S. nation building as well as the use of history itself as a literal and epistemological place-maker to assert belonging. Goeman explains how "the dialectic of stories in the past and present break from the unidirectional, progressive narrative found in the narratives of manifest destiny. Indigenous conceptions of land are literally and figuratively the placeholder that moves through time and situates [I]ndigenous knowledges."[33] The site becomes a way of not dismissing the past so as to move forward into the future, but of rereading the past as well as the present and future through Dakota perspective.

Resisting Containment

The Dakota story of this place resists being confined to and/or constituted by settler colonialist designations or meanings. Upon entering the site from the visitor's parking lot, the complexity of the site and the sense of multiple meanings are immediately evident. Just off the parking lot is a post titled "Welcome to Historic Fort Snelling." It reads, "[t]wo miles to the east of this spot, the powerful Mississippi and Minnesota Rivers merge. This is a site of creation for Dakota people. These are the ancestral homelands to other Native nations and have been for more than 10,000 years." The connection to Bdote, "two miles east of this spot" along with phrases "[t]his is a site of creation for Dakota people" and "[t]hese are the ancestral homelands" make distinguishing the exact location and its parameters of "the site of Dakota creation" difficult. Is the site of Dakota creation "two miles east" or, as indicated by "this is a site," where the visitor stands? The idea that fixing or limiting the site of Dakota creation is further complicated by the words "these are the ancestral homelands." By linguistically placing the first reference to Dakota "two miles upstream," but then also using phrases "this spot" and "these are the ancestral homelands," it is left unclear as to whether the Dakota originated at Bdote two miles upstream, the location of the post itself, and/or the larger area. The inclusion of references to the site as being Bdote, though with no specific reference points or boundaries, reflects a rejection of what Coulthard explains as "a rejection of the profoundly asymmetrical and non-reciprocal forms of recognition granted to them by the colonial-state society."[34] This linguistic and visual framing or placing works to assert Dakota place and makes fully understanding it rely on Dakota logics. In this way, Dakota connections to this place are asserted via, but not subsumed by, MNHS. This reflects Simpson's discussion of how "refusal" rejects the mapping or naming by MNHS, and in doing so, reflects "radical resurgence."[35]

The first installation visitors see after the "Welcome to Historic Fort Snelling" post is a large interactive installation quoting part of the 1805 Treaty , also known as Pike's Treaty. A post which visitors encounter before the entirety of the larger installation asks the question, "Why do Treaties Matter?" It answers the question:

> Treaties are binding agreements between sovereign nations. While both the federal government and Dakota leaders later questioned the validity of this treaty, the United States never renounced the claim to 100,000 acres. The 1805 treaty land eventually became parts of Minneapolis and St. Paul.
>
> Whether you are Dakota or not, the 1805 treaty affects your life today. As the first of 16 treaties between the United States and the Dakota and Ojibwe nations, it started a process of massive land loss for Native people that opened most of Minnesota up for settlement. It was also the first step toward Dakota exile.

The placement of this post, prior to being able to fully read and contemplate the meaning of the 1805 treaty, invites the visitor to position themselves in relation to the treaty and its implications. The statement "whether you are Dakota or not, the 1805 treaty affects your life today," makes it clear that the treaty affects the visitor not only as they identify as Dakota or not but also as they stand in this space. By naming Dakota first, this wording positions Dakota to be the primary, though not exclusive, visitor to the site. This discursive and material privileging of Dakota highlights as well as interrupts the role that this and other treaties play in undermining Indigenous agency.

The ability of visitors to contemplate how they are affected by the treaty is complicated by the interplay of light and dark shading and angles in the piece. The post reads, "The United States promises on their part to permit the Sioux to pass, repass, hunt, or make other uses of said [d]istricts, as they have formerly done." The juxtaposition of light and dark metal lines upon which each letter of the words is placed makes reading it from start to finish impossible. The words, "The United States," "on their part," "the Sioux," and "or make other uses of said districts" are on lighter background, making the words easier to read. In contrast, the words, "promises," "to permit," and "to pass, repass, hunt," are on the darker panels, making them more difficult to read. Further, the darker panels are angled so that the light catches these sections of words differently. The bench and gravel invite visitors to move around to read the words from different angles. Indeed, one must move around and reposition oneself to read all of the words. All of these elements make a streamlined reading of the treaty impossible. Indeed, they highlight the role that positionality plays in how one reads and understands this text. It disturbs the long-held and dominant settler colonialist reading of the treaty and asserts Dakota interpretation and perspective. Together, these material and discursive elements foreground the irreconcilability of the two interpretations of the treaty.

As one moves through the site and into the larger space, Dakota land relations are more evident. "A Place to Remember" invites multiple interpretations of the site. The space is set back from the main walkway between the visitor's center and the rebuilt fort, and is just off of the walkway that runs behind the visitor's center and overlooks the Mississippi River. A simple post reads "All are welcome here," and below it, "A place to remember. To pay tribute to the many lives shaped by this place and the generations who lived, labored, and learned here. To recognize the pain, loss, and sacrifice of those connected to this place." With no specific people, nation, or events cited, the signage insists that the place itself be the focus. The focus on the place is evident in the wording "shaped by *this place*," "generations who lived, labored, and learned *here*," "of those connected to *this place*." While the timeframe moves between past and present, the focus on place is fixed.

While the immediate focus is on remembering or past-looking, the signification of the place, as told in "a place to remember," is not confined to the past. The break between the past and present is annulled via the act of remembering. The highlighting of place privileges it over time. The demarcating of place according to time thereby becomes irrelevant. This is evident in the phrases "to remember," "the many lives shaped by this place," as well as the "pain, loss, and sacrifice" of those connected to this place. The focus on "those connected to this place" highlights the present. While "generations" is past-looking, "those connected to this place" is present-looking. While there is a discursive movement between past, present, and future, the focus on place is fixed and central. The ease of movement in time is echoed in the visual aesthetics. Below these words, starting at the very bottom of the post, are shaded figures of tall prairie grasses. The fact that they are similar in height, size, and shape to the living plants surrounding the sign breaks the barrier between past and present, here and not here, living and dead. The shading and colors of the plants on the sign create a sense that they could sway in the breeze, just like the living ones surrounding them.

In the center of the space are seven square sandstone boulders in a circle. They resemble the Council Fires Overlook, seven sandstone markers just across the Minnesota River at Oheyawahi (Pilot Knob Hill) that are engraved with the names of the seven tribes that make up the Dakota, Lakota, and Nakota nations.[36] The stones at the fort, though, are not labeled. Only those visitors who know the significance of seven, whether by virtue of having visited Oheyawahi and/or having knowledge of the Dakota Oyate, might infer that they represent the seven nations. Understanding the stones as representative of the seven nations reflects what Goeman explains as a way to call out the significance of place and not time. Goeman writes, "[c]onceiving of space as a node rather than a linear time construct marked by supposed shifting ownerships is a powerful mechanism in resisting imperial geographies that order time and space in hierarchies that erase and busy [I]ndigenous connections to place and anesthetize settler colonial histories."[37] The stones convey a sense of enduring despite the constructing and reconstructing of settler spaces all around them. They reflect the endearment to and endurance of Indigenous space over time. Without these stones being labeled, the visitor is free to attach any significance/signification to the stones and the ground on which they rest. In this way, the Indigenous significance of these stones is not determined by or contained within the signage or narrative of the site offered by MNHS. This is in sharp contrast to the older, more worn placards between the "Place to Remember" and the fort structure.

Older placards represent Dakota and the fort only in relation to the U.S.-Dakota war. These older placards are distinct from the newer installations as evidenced by their chipped paint, sun-bleached façade, and older font. Situated on either side of a tarred path between the visitor's center and the rebuilt fort, they are interspersed by a bike rack and bench. The placement of the signs along the path and near the bike intersection disincline visitors from pausing much longer than the time needed to read the placards. The busy Highway 55, which runs underneath the site, can be seen from this spot as well. The first two placards visitors encounter focus on the "U.S.-Dakota War of 1862" and the "Imprisonment of Dakota Families." The panel just across the walk, "Imprisonment of Dakota Families," states that "in this concentration camp, Dakota families endured crowding, hunger, and disease over the winter of 1862–63. As many as 300 people died." The panel just next to this, "Executions at Fort Snelling," includes a picture of Ṡakṗe and Wakan Ożaŋżaŋ, two Dakota men who were executed at the fort in November 1865. Past the bike rack and bench is another permanent placard referencing St. Peter's Indian Agency, which, as the placard explains, stood just a block or so from the fort.[38] Their placement, particularly at this busy intersection of walking and bike paths, makes their inclusion seem somewhat requisite and forced.

This is in sharp contrast to "A Quiet Place to Remember," which can only be accessed by getting off of the walking path and entering the circled space. The "war" placards narrow the Dakota connection to the site in terms of war and death. In contrast, while "A Place to Remember" doesn't bar remembrances of the 1820s to the 1860s, it also does not limit the space to this meaning. The placement, accessibility, and written and visual aesthetics in "A Place to Remember" invites and holds space for visitors to contemplate multiple meanings of the site. Past the older placards is the rebuilt fort and the Fort Snelling State Park administrated by the Minnesota Department of Natural Resources (DNR).

In addition to abbreviated and disjointed narrative of Dakota at the site, there is a somewhat abrupt break between the MNHS site and the site administrated by the DNR. The cement walking path to the main entrance of the fort is bisected by a gravel path and a set of older cement stairs. While this path is marked on the Historic Fort brochure, the sign indicating that this is the path to the state park is visible only after one has turned down and around the fort and walked about 150 feet. The abrupt break between the MNHS site and the DNR state park conveys a disjointedness, or the sense that neither MNHS or the DNR can fully convey the story of this place.[39] The Dakota meanings are evident in the fissures and cracks of these two disjointed sites as well as the signage therein.

Dakota Refusal and Recognition

This chapter has explored how Indigenous refusal and recognition are negotiated within settler colonialist state logics. The Bdote Memory Map relies on images, videos, pictures, and voices of Dakota speakers explaining the importance of these places. These maps are held by Dakota. The digital Bdote Memory Map as well as the signage at Bdote represent what Betasamosake Simpson explains as the "maps those Elders carried in their bodies as two-dimensional representations of the networks they live and their parents and grandparents lived."[40] The meanings of these places cannot be fully demarcated on a map; one comes to them through listening, learning, and being in relation with those who share them. From its first articulation by Mona Smith at Ancient Trader's Gallery, to the online memory map, and Bdote itself, the map represents an insistence on Dakota place relations and negotiation of settler colonialist terms of recognition. It reflects what Simpson explains as a "refusal" to rely on non-Dakota "recognition paradigms" for "rendering justice." Further, through this Indigenous analysis of the Historic Fort Snelling at Bdote, the inability of non-Indigenous place logics to fully articulate Indigenous place logics is made evident. Additionally, the literal and figurative parameters of the fort, the ways in which it must constantly rebuild and retell its story, stand in sharp contrast to Dakota place relations which do not require replicas and reenactments.

In seeking to tell more of the stories of the site, and including thereby more Dakota resources to tell those stories, settler colonialism makes visible the terms by which itself is constituted. In the spring 2023 update to the Historic Fort Snelling website, the "Bdote" page includes a link to the Bdote Memory Map. The inclusion of this map, within the virtual space of Historic Fort Snelling, works to make visible what Snelgrove, Dhamoon, and Corntassel explain as a "space of resistance." The map reflects the complexity and contradictions in settler colonialist frames of recognition. The inclusion of Dakota narratives on the site, narratives and connections that existed prior to settlement, makes visible the relationship with this site that existed and endures prior to and despite settler colonialism. Settler colonialist narratives of place must be reconstituted via the rebuilding and continued maintenance of the fort. That these material, visual, and discursive stories of settlement must be preserved and makes visible the instabilities and precarities of national narratives.

Simpson writes about how consent and refusal work in terms of the state representing Indigenous voices. She explains how the forgetting of Indigenous peoples is:

> challenged by the counter that Indigenous people represent simply by (1) living and (b) knowing this. In living and knowing themselves as such, they post a demand upon the newness of the present, as well as a knotty reminder of something else.

> That "something else" is the ongoing work of dispossession, and its handmaiden of failed assimilation.[41]

The images of Neerdaels teaching children outside and the teachings of elders as well as videos of the sites all reflect Simpson's argument of how the forgetting of Indigenous peoples is challenged by "(a) living and (b) knowing this." The Bdote Memory Map site makes this knowing evident and, in the circulation of that knowledge, expands it. Users become complicit in the knowing of the Dakota significance of this place. In knowing, users are constituted as part of this resistance to settler colonialist logics.

The Bdote map builds on as well as complicates users' understandings of these places.[42] The Bdote Memory Map makes evident and accessible the ways in which Dakota spaces and the terms of being and belonging in those spaces are always already present. The Bdote Memory Map relies, to a great extent, on user engagement; users have to open and navigate the maps/sites to a specific place. As such, these maps invite users to identify the places of greatest significance to the user, albeit through the lens of Dakota relationship to them. This interface reflects and reinforces the users' agency in identifying places of significance. It reflects Dickinson's argument that "rhetorical investigations of material place will nearly always involve us in the complex, unsettled, unstable, porous, and often surprising relations between the efforts to shut down and expand agency."[43] The Bdote Memory Map makes visible and accessible Dakota agency insofar as Dakota meanings are layered over and/or alongside other meanings of these spaces.

Refusal is evident throughout, but particularly in places such as demarcations on maps, the ways the words and images on the signs, as well as their placement and surrounding area all indicate the significance of the site as Dakota. This makes Simpson's point about competing sovereignties most evident both as Dakota folks live it and as interpretation or framing of space reflects it. Dakota relation to the site is made evident, but it resists foreclosure or parameters. At the same time, the specificity of the MNHS site is much more apparent, and as such, so are its chronological and spatial parameters. All of this exposes the ways settler colonialist significance is grafted onto the site. As such, it makes the precariousness of settler colonialism most evident. Simpson writes about how the Iroquois national lacrosse player case makes visible how they and all Indigenous nations:

> remind nation-states such as the United States (and Canada) that they possess this very history, and within that history and seized space, they possess a precarious assumption that their boundaries are permanent, uncontestable, and entrenched. They possess a precarious assumption about their own (just) origins. And by extension, they possess a precarious assumption about themselves.[44]

Close study of the efforts over time to rebuild, restore, and re-mark reveals how these efforts expose the "precarious presumption" held by the state.

Conclusion

Dare I say anything that's not a Native person being forced off their land is a flag upgrade? Excited to have a new state flag that represents every Minnesotan.

—Anishinaabekwe, Lt. Governor of Minnesota, Peggy Flanagan, X, December 19, 2023

It may seem odd that a celebration of the new state flag design focuses not on what had been added to this prominent symbol of the state, but rather what has been removed. For those who have followed the public discussion surrounding the Minnesota state flag and seal, though, Lieutenant Governor Peggy Flanagan's tweet is no surprise.[1] Flanagan's reference to "anything that's not a Native person being forced off their land" is reference to a central and prominent part of the now former state flag and seal.

The former Minnesota state flag and seal tell one story of Minnesota in which farmer settlers till the ground and Indigenous peoples move west. In the foreground is a farmer facing eastward tilling the ground with a rifle slung on a nearby tree stump. In the background is an Indigenous man, on horseback, riding westward. The three dates in the circle around the image are the establishment of Fort Snelling in 1819, statehood in 1858, and the year the original flag design was adopted in 1893. In 1858, first state governor, Henry Sibley, added "L'etoile du nord," "Star of the North."[2] It is clear that many believe this is the story of Minnesota and therefore should remain on the flag.[3] The flag discussion in Minnesota is similar to conversations about public memory taking place across the United States.

The creation and later revisions of the state flag and seal occurred during pivotal times in which the state of Minnesota, and the country, were negotiating racial tensions. The seal and flag were originally designed and authorized in 1858 and 1861.[4] Henry Sibley, then territorial governor, oversaw the design of the seal and later flag.[5] Sibley was central to land treaties in Dakota and Ojibwe lost millions of acres of land.[6] The seal and flag were reauthorized in 1958. This time was the beginning of a period of great racial upheaval and change beginning with *Brown v. Board of Education* in 1954.[7] The Indian Relocation Act (P.L. 959) also occurred in 1956, which brought thousands of Indigenous people to major cities like Minneapolis and Saint Paul with promises of job training, housing, and education.[8] Prior to 2023, the last time the state of Minnesota revisited the flag and seal, it did so during a time in which Black and Indigenous people were gaining visibility that they heretofore had not had. The reaffirmation of a by-then century-old version of farming and Indigenous movement west reaffirmed white agrarian settlement and Indigenous removal. The former stage flag and seal, like many of the confederate monuments around the country, were originally designed and a century later affirmed at a time when communities of color were gaining visibility and civil rights.

Recent years have also seen great racial upheaval and turmoil and, like previous eras, there is a strain of public sentiment that seeks to preserve a specific narrative of people and place. In 2018, the Southern Poverty Law Center identified "1,747 Confederate monuments, place names, and other symbols still in public spaces." The report cites events such as the 2015 killing of nine people at a historic Black church in Charleston, South Carolina, by a white supremacist and the prominence of the confederate flag in the killer's social media posts as "a moment of deep reflection for the nation."[9] The report was released just two years before the killing of George Floyd at the hands of a Minneapolis police officer.[10] These prominent events ushered in conversations about the role of public symbols and the ways in which they reflect and uphold ideologues and ideologies of racial genocide.[11]

It is not just symbols of the confederacy, but also that of Christopher Columbus that have come under broader scrutiny.[12] While the image of protestors tearing down the Columbus statue in front of the Minnesota state capital made national news, this was not the first time or instance that Columbus and the relationship between Black and Indigenous genocide was made. Instances of Columbus statues being taken down and/or vandalized include Richmond, Virginia; Boston, Massachusetts; Miami, Florida; and other places.[13] In a photo spread titled "The Statues Brought Down Since the George Floyd Protests Began," *The Atlantic* grouped confederate and Columbus statutes together in those "targeted" "as voices rose against historic and systemic racism and oppression."[14] Lieutenant Governor Peggy Flanagan gave a news conference following the tearing down of the Columbus statue on the grounds of the Minnesota state capital. She stated, "I'm not going to perform for folks. I'm not going to feign sadness. I will not shed a tear over the loss of a statue that honored someone that by of his own admission sold nine- and ten-year-old girls into sex slavery. So, let us start there."[15] Flanagan's words are extraordinary because she, as Indigenous woman herself, names the harm committed by Columbus on Indigenous girls and women. Further, by stating, "let us start there," Flanagan insists that the welfare of Indigenous girls and women be the first criteria in evaluating the worthiness of the monument.

Failure to fully acknowledge the past undermines our collective abilities and willingness to see Indigenous peoples in the past and the present. As Kim TallBear explains in the NPR *Code Switch* piece, "The Standing Rock Resistance Is Unprecedented (It's Also Centuries Old)":

> Maybe for non-Natives who thought that the West was won, and the Indian Wars were over, and Native people were mostly dead and gone and isn't that too bad—now, they're like, "Oh wait a minute, they're still there? And they're still fighting the same things they were 150 years ago?" Yeah, we are.[16]

TallBear's argument that Indigenous folks are "still fighting for the same things" echoes Flanagan's insistence that the fight to have Indigeneity and Indigenous rights recognized is just as prescient today as it was 150 years ago. Indigenous women and girls continue to be victims of violence at rates significantly higher than other ethnic or racial groups.[17] Also, perpetrators are overwhelmingly non-Indigenous. At the center of these fights, whether honoring treaties at Standing Rock or insisting that the health and safety of Indigenous women and girls be recognized, is a demand to be seen. It is a demand to have land disputes like Standing Rock and public monuments seen through Indigenous epistemologies. The failure to recognize the harm to Indigenous peoples in the past, committed by Columbus and the like, is akin to the same failure to recognize the harms being committed in the present. This is about compelling the greater public to examine the past and the present through Indigenous eyes.

For many, the former Minnesota state flag represented the genocide of Minnesota's Indigenous peoples. At a May 2023 commission hearing, Upper Sioux Community tribal chairperson Kevin Jensvold explained why he speaks up about the need to change the flag. Jensvold stated:

> I represent 549 tribal members. Two hundred and four of them are less than the age of eighteen who, who, in this day and age, need to be talked for, need to be protected, need to be stood up for, need to be defended. One of them asked me, why is there a gun pointed at the Indian head? And so I will disagree with Representative Freiberg that twenty of these [state] flags are very similar cause I don't know how many of those flags show a gun pointed at Indian.[18]

Jensvold's sharing how young Indigenous children read the flag and seal reflects how this image of the past informs the present. It is easy to bemoan the loss of this image if it is read only through farmer settler eyes. Though, read through Indigenous eyes, as the words of the children Jensvold shares, the image represents and reinforces harm to and the removal of Indigenous peoples. The effort to select a new flag and seal is, as Jensvold and Flanagan argue, about ensuring that all Minnesotans see themselves reflected in it. Both Indigenous and non-Indigenous Minnesotans have spoken out about the need to change the flag.

Minnesota State Representative Mike Freiberg is co-author of Minnesota House File 274, a bill to create a commission to solicit and select a new flag design. Representative Freiberg argued that "it is very consciously part of the design of the seal to depict the displacement of Native Americans, and I don't think it has any place on our state flag."[19] It is important to note that the desire for a new flag, as stated by Minnesota Senator Mary Kunesh, first Indigenous woman to serve in the Minnesota state Senate, is about accurate representation. As Kunesh explained to *MPR News*, "[l]ook at how our Native folks have persevered and stayed connected with the culture and the religion and the language, and the land appreciation," she said. "We have been here, we are here, and we're still contributing to the health and wealth of Minnesota."[20] In many ways, the work of Freiberg, Kunesh, and other members of the flag committee is to envision how this central symbol of the state can tell a more complete story of this place and all its people.

This book has explored how Indigenous activism at the sites of and in the discourses about history assert Indigeneity as well as expose and explicate settler colonialism. Indigenous place relations are about existing, resisting, and persisting. Indigenous activism therefore asserts that Indigenous connection with place is about knowledge of and relationship with both the place and others who share that relationship. Because these relationships must be asserted more or less through settler colonialist institutions, Indigenous activists must negotiate the available terms of representation. These negotiated refusals, as Indigenous scholars have argued, can result in radical resurgence. By rejecting representation via logics of place and time, by refusing to fix land relations to a specific time, Indigeneity makes itself known. Further, this refusal to be contained within material and discursive rhetoric of place asserts Indigenous land relations as ever present. Indigenous place relations do not require posted signs and storylines. They exist within the relations with the place. This is in sharp contrast to settler colonialist place relations.

Although settler colonialist land relations may certainly be felt and remembered, they are ultimately bound by place and time. This focus on place and time is what positions logics of ownership as paramount. These contracts of belonging are then reinforced via memory sites like those at Historic Fort Snelling and The Landing. Together, they maintain the dominant logics of state and economies and the privileges afforded therein. Settler colonialism must constantly reinscribe itself onto places deemed to have historical importance. Settler colonialism resuscitates moments in time and events of white settlement and Indigenous removal in order to reassure itself of its connection to place. In this way, it reflects a sort of *Weekend at Bernie's* resuscitation of settler life and settlement.[21] In sharp contrast, Indigenous land relations exist within Indigenous communities and therefore do not require reanimation. By holding these two epistemologies up to each other and examining them through the lens of Indigenous place relations, these underlying logics are more readily exposed. Indigenous activism is therefore not only an assertion of this relationship but, as an always already existing logic of place, it unavoidably exposes and interrogates settler colonialist place relations. Indigenous place relations invite ways of seeing place that are not bound by settler colonialism.

Grounded Normativity as Indigenous Activism

This discussion has centered on land not only because I have examined places of historic significance, but the places themselves hold great significance to the Dakota nation and settler farmer memory of the state of Minnesota. Indigenous studies scholars echo the argument that land is central to Indigenous existence. While place is a touchpoint and source of that relation, it functions both as a place of significance but also as an ontology that informs how to interact. As an ontology, it is not subject (or less subject to) the whims the state in naming and organizing. It resists and remains within the Indigenous community that holds that relation. The power of the examples I have explored is that by examining them as assertions of Indigeneity first and foremost, the ways in which they expose and explicate settler colonialism is made particularly evident. Indigenous communities staking their existence at the sites in which it is challenged especially works to "out" settler colonialism as the epistemologies that are grafted onto place and thereby require periodic restructuring. When Indigenous activists seize upon these moments, they make visible these loose threads. Indigenous land relations do not require this maintenance of narrative told through and about place.

In Indigenous terms, belonging and being Indigenous are constituted via a relationship with the land. Indigenous studies scholar Betasamosake Simpson explains "Nishnaabeg intelligence" as:

> a theoretical anchor that transforms over time and space within individual and collective Nishnaabeg consciousness. . . . "Theory" is regenerated continually through embodied practice and within each family, community and generation of people. "Theory" isn't just an intellectual pursuit—it is woven within kinetics, spiritual presence and emotion, it is contextual and relational.[22]

Land is generative of knowledge, of people. In Indigenous or grounded normativity, land is the center of everything, one's identity and spirituality are created and sustained through a relationship with land. Land is not a means or a resource through which to construct or derive one's identity, as it is in settler colonialist terms.

Centering analysis on land to explore settler colonialism and Indigenous activism makes particularly evident the machinations of settler colonialism as well as the ways in which Indigeneity "exists, resists, and persists."[23] Land, as Indigenous studies scholar Mishuanna Goeman explains, holds the past, present, and future as one. She writes:

> Indigenous conceptions of land are literally and figuratively the placeholder that moves through time and situates indigenous knowledges. Conceiving of space as a node rather than a linear time construct marked by supposed shifting ownerships is a powerful mechanism in resisting imperial geographies that order space and time in hierarchies that erase and bury indigenous connections to place and anesthetize settler-colonial histories.[24]

Holding land central to discussions of settlement and Indigeneity makes especially visible the ways in which settlement stories of land work to anesthetize the genocidal components of settlement. Examining arguments about land through Indigenous theories makes visible how Indigenous land relations remain and resist.

Understood this way, Indigenous activism is a reflection and demonstration of love for one's land and those who hold the same relationship with it. Betasamosake Simpson explains how "intense love of land, of family, and of our nations that has always been the spine of Indigenous resistance." She continues, "we need to join together in a rebellion of love, persistence, commitment, and profound caring and create constellations of coresistance, working together toward a radical alternative present based on deep reciprocity and the gorgeous generative refusal of colonial recognition."[25] Reading Indigenous activism as simply a response to settler colonialism and its infractions is shortsighted and therefore inaccurate. A more accurate understanding of Indigenous activism is that it is ever present; it is something that is brought into wider visibility when Indigenous communities assert their connection to land. Further, it is not a positioning against or retaliation of the machinations of settler colonialism, but rather a gesture of love and resilience with and for the Indigenous community.

Through these case studies, I have explored Indigenous activism, which is grounded normativity, on its own terms. Writing about her work, Simpson speaks of her excitement in building on Indigenous studies scholar Glen Coulthard's reading of Fanon from simply "turning away" to "the range of possibilities available for political life, for identification and identity within and against recognition, all instantiated in refusals."[26] The "within and against recognition" thus is not only a matter of examining Indigenous activism as it reflects Indigenous communities, but it is a matter of using the terms of recognition as they are articulated by and emerge from within the community itself to examine the contours of public activism. Analysis, therefore, is not a matter of how Indigenous communities challenge the actions or logics of the settler state, but rather how Indigenous communities continually reassert their own logics through their actions.

Read as a reflection of grounded normativity, it becomes clear that Indigenous activism takes many different forms. While some Indigenous activism is highly visible, such as that at the Walker Sculpture Garden, that activism is only one, albeit prominent, assertion of an already existent connection to that place. Writing about a June 2009 community march in Nogojiwanong, Betasamosake Simpson writes:

> [t]his was not a protest, This was not a demonstration. This was a quiet, collective act of resurgence. It was a mobilization and it was political because it was a reminder. It was a reminder that although we are collectively unseen in the city of Peterborough, when we come together with one mind and one heart we can transform our land and our city into a decolonized space and a place of resurgence, even if it is for a brief amount of time.[27]

While events like that which occurred at the Walker compel Indigenous activists to assert it, Indigenous land relations endure. Activism is therefore not simply a rejection of representation through a settler colonialist lens but what Betasamosake Simpson calls a "radical resurgence." Staying with the activism at the Walker, the event was not simply a rejection of isolation of the Dakota community to December 26, 1862. Just as, if not more, importantly, it was an assertion of the Dakota community and its continued existence and ever-present connection to this land. In this way, refusal is generative—it brings into visibility (not being) Indigenous land relations.

Negotiating Refusal and Resurgence

By centering grounded normativity in this analysis, I have made more visible the nuances and tensions that inform Indigenous agency as it works within and outside of settler colonialist institutions. These case studies position us to think about Betasamosake Simpson's discussion of "radical resurgence" and the distinction she makes between resurgence that leaves the neoliberal policies and possessions of the state intact and those that restore and reaffirm Indigenous land relation both as an ontology and as a lived experience. Betasamosake Simpson writes, "I am not interested in inclusion. I am not interested in reconciling. I'm interested in unapologetic place-based nationhoods using Indigenous practices and operating in an ethical and principled way from an intact land base."[28] Evaluated through this lens, Makoce Ikikcupi most reflects radical resurgence.

The Makoce Ikikcupi project's focus on using the site as a way to bring back exiled relatives reflects the "unapologetic place-based nationhoods" of which Betasamosake Simpson writes. The project asserts that Dakota land relations predate and therefore usurp those of the state of Minnesota and the United States. As such, it reflects the endurance of Dakota nationhood as well as what constitutes nationhood. Dakota nationhood, unlike settler colonial nationhood, which is based on property, is based on land relations. Makoce Ikikcupi is almost entirely outside the purview or authority of state and economic institutions.[29] This is in contrast to sites like Historical Fort Snelling at Bdote where access to the site and management of it are under the logistical and ontological control of the Minnesota Historical Society as well as the Minnesota Department of Natural Resources and the National Park Service.[30]

Refusal is evident in Makoce Ikikcupi and Historic Fort Snelling at Bdote. As Simpson writes, the counter to the state and the mechanisms of dispossession, both of land and lifeways, is refusal. Refusal, though, is not dependent upon recognition by the state. Rather, refusal in the context of Indigeneity can also be simply being. It is, as Simpson writes, "living" and "being." She continues, "[r]efusal is a symptom, a practice, a possibility for doing things differently, for thinking beyond the recognition paradigm that is the agreed-upon "antidote" for rendering justice in deeply unequal scenes of articulation."[31] Makoce Ikikcupi's focus on securing land so as to practice Dakota culture reflects the "living" and "being" of which Simpson speaks.

Refusal is also evident at Historic Fort Snelling at Bdote in the placement of Dakota references being almost entirely outside of the rebuilt fort. In this way, Dakota presence and land connection is asserted almost exclusively in those spaces that have not been rebuilt. Dakota resist being fully represented in and on the terms of the historical society. The newer installation references to Dakota convey a horizon of meaning. It invites visitors to identify the literal and figurative terms through which they identify and navigate the space. It invites meaning beyond that which is immediately evident. It does not limit or foreclose interpretations of the site to those which are presently offered. It does, though, stand outside of these logics. It announces Indigeneity on its own terms. Ultimately, the forced materiality of the settler colonialist site makes visible the constructedness of the site and strict adherence to a single, linear, and finite narrative. This refusal to be confined to a specific time is a crucial part of asserting Indigeneity.

Indigenous peoples are caught in needing to articulate land relations or otherwise risk being folded into historical narratives of genocide and removal. *Scaffold* was a rhetorical exigence that demanded a response. The moment required an assertion of continuous Dakota existence as well as a rejection of the terms of recognition offered via *Scaffold.* Instead of simply working literally and figuratively within the institution of the Walker and the Minneapolis Parks Board, activists used the outdoor space to refuse recognition on the Walker, Viso, and Durant's terms. By insisting that the 38+2 be recognized as part of a larger and living community, the activists rejected genocide in all its forms—both as representative and literal. They instead used that space as one of radical resurgence. The short- and long-term effects of this activism allow us to consider Dakota recognition and its implications for the later site.

These tensions and how Indigenous voices navigated them are evident in the changes at the Walker. The structure was taken down, Angela Two Stars's *Okciyapi* was constructed, and other Indigenous-centered events were held.[32] The lingering question, though, is to what extent is settler colonialism exposed and challenged throughout the organization? Simpson explains the "slippery" nature of recognition insofar as it "is only performed, however, if the problem of cultural difference and alterity does not pose too appalling a challenge to the norms of settler society."[33] The new installation, and particularly its focus on Dakota language being written and spoken as well as water, reflects regeneration. The language, water, and relation to this place has always been here; the installation reflects and reinvigorates this. The lack of instant translation to

English reflects a rejection of being neatly folded into English/settler colonialist systems. The water and the Dakota language are a constant, fixed, articulation of Dakota land relations. As such, the sculpture not only interrupts a uniform interpretation of the site, but it casts into question the ordering of logics used to populate and narrate the larger site.

Dakota land relations are most fully realized at Makoce Ikikcupi. Betasamosake Simpson's desire for "place-based nationhoods using Indigenous practices and operating in an ethical and principled way from an in-tact land base" is most reflected in Makoce Ikikcupi. The project's focus on this particular land as the basis of and holding "spiritual and physical relationship" reflects Betasamosake Simpson's desire for Indigenous communities "operating in an ethical and principled way from an intact land base." This also goes back to Coulthard's argument that Indigenous communities seek to "critically evaluate, reconstruct and redeploy culture."[34] The resurgence of Dakota culture on this site as a way to bring exiled relatives home reflects the importance of an "in-tact land base." Conceptions of land and whose conceptions hold sway over the control and management of land is the heart of this discussion.

The fundamental challenge to assertions of Indigenous being is that many of the sites of significance, such as Bdote and The Landing, are administrated by governmental institutions. Since institutions such as the MNHS and the Minnesota DNR are arms of the state government, settler colonialism is baked into their founding and guiding ideologies. Left to articulate being within these larger logics of settler colonialism, Indigenous assertions of being are tenuous. Indigeneity must negotiate terms of recognition without having their identity partially or fully subsumed by the institution's logics. In this way, Indigenous people are faced with a catch-22 of sorts. Indigeneity and Indigenous communities must assert their being and belonging at places of significance lest they become fodder for roads, homes, or businesses.[35] Yet, the degree to which state institutions can recognize Indigeneity or Indigenous peoples as they themselves articulate their land relations is questionable. At best, Indigenous peoples and land relations are never fully represented and at worst Indigenous peoples and places are harmed. The newer installations at Historic Fort Snelling and Three Rivers Park reflect the ways in which Indigeneity makes itself known while resisting being folded into or subsumed by settler colonialist logics of time and place. These case studies have made visible some of the tensions at play in Indigenous refusal and resurgence.

Indigenous Mobilities

Another aspect of Indigenous activism is diaspora and mobility. The negative impacts of Indigenous diaspora have long been recognized, most recently with the release of the Department of the Interior's final report on Federal Indian Boarding Schools.[36] The examples of Indigenous activism I have explored here, though, make visible how contemporary Indigenous peoples have marshalled forced relocation and other methods of diaspora into networks of Indigenous activism. The case studies I have examined elucidate the strategies used by Indigenous activists working within their own tribal nations, inter-tribally, with non-Indigenous allies, as well as within and between urban and rural areas. This reflects Betasamosake Simpson's argument that instead of framing Indigeneity solely as a matter of diaspora, it is more productive to think in terms of "mobility." She writes, "mobility shatters and refuses the containment of settler colonialism and inserts Indigenous presence. This is an asset." Mobility, Betasamosake Simpson says, can take four different forms. It is "an embedded Indigenous practice, mobility as a response to colonial resistance, mobility as deliberate and strategic resurgence, and mobility as direct or indirect forced expulsion, relocation, and displacement and the creation of Indigenous diaspora."[37] As these case studies have demonstrated, mobility is a significant part of Indigenous activism.

Mobility is a reflection of what Indigenous peoples have always known. Mobility as "an embedded Indigenous practice" is evident in the Bdote Memory Maps. Visitors to Mona Smith's installation brought with them the knowledge to build the maps. Smith's work made what was already evident and shareable between Dakota community members and others. Indigenous knowledge is evident in Makoce Ikikcupi, as the creation and maintenance of the site relies on Dakota land knowledge. Finally, mobility as an "embedded Indigenous practice" is evident at Historic Fort Snelling at Bdote. Interpreting and navigating the site requires Dakota land knowledge. Visitors to the site, therefore, do not rely on signage or built installations, but rely instead on what they and their community already know. Accessing this information therefore can only be done as part of a relationship with Dakota. The relationship precedes the knowledge, as opposed to shared knowledge preceding relationship building.

Mobility as a resource is evident in the activism at the Walker and Mona Smith's installation. Smith's piece, created shortly after the violence of the

Minneapolis police, was a direct response to and resignification of police violence. Police violence and the celebration of genocide are examples of colonial resistance that Smith and the activism the Walker responded to. The rapid and thoughtful response to *Scaffold* of both advocacy within the Walker and outside of it was a "deliberate and strategic" response to "colonial resistance." Finally, mobility as "deliberate and strategic" is evident in the short- and long-term planning at Makoce Ikikcupi. The mission of the site, both for short-term projects and long term with the significance of re-establishing Dakota land relations and lifeways to bring more Dakota home, is central.

Finally, mobility as diaspora is evident in each of the case studies as well. The "direct or indirect forced expulsion, relocation, and displacement" was evident in the urban setting of the gallery where Smith's work was hosted. The American Indian corridor, where many Indigenous reestablished tribal and inter-tribal communities as a result of the Indian Urbanization Act of 1956, is now a thriving cultural and economic center. Makoce Ikikcupi is a response to the forced expulsion of Dakota from the state. And Historic Fort Snelling at Bdote makes visible the expulsion of Dakota by the state as well as the continued connection of Dakota to the site. Recognizing the many forms of mobility evident in these case studies demonstrates the need to further explore the significance of Indigenous diaspora as part of contemporary Indigenous activism even as the assertion of place relations is central that that activism.

Seeing Place, Seeing All People

Looking closely at the non-Indigenous allies like John Stoesz and his work with Makoce Ikikcupi and those that participated in the action at the Walker, it becomes evident that it is not only Indigenous peoples that seek recognition outside of settler colonialist logics. Two handmade signs from the activism at the Walker reflect a multi-prong assertion of ethnicities and sexualities outside of settler colonialism. Both signs reflect the role of settler colonialism as it imposes heteronormativity on bodies and romantic relationships. On one, the words "queer Hmong US-Created Refugee" reflects the role of settler colonialism as it organizes not just land, but also bodies into frames of intelligibility. Just as settler colonialism created queer identity through the imposition of the gender binary, it created refugees through the imposition of state making. In this way, the 1973 Hmong refugee is akin to the 1863 Dakota refugee. This is echoed on the other sign with the flag and writing "two-spirit." "Two-spirit" is the term that Indigenous communities use to reclaim the cultural norm of recognizing and valuing multiple genders and sexual orientations. The imposition of the gender and sex binary is a product of settler colonialism.[38] The activism at the Walker, therefore, asserted two-spirit peoples and exposed machinations of settler colonialism insofar as it organized land and bodies.

Focusing on Indigenous land relations works to reorientate our thinking about land, people, and place. Indigenous studies scholar Lisa King explains in her examination of Bishop Museum in Honolulu how "through a reorientation toward the values and epistemologies of the Indigenous nation on whose land the Bishop Museum rests, there are possibilities for more fully recognizing the way that colonialism is still at work and the ways that alliances might be found."[39] Centering or beginning conversations about place with the Indigenous knowledges and communities of that place unsettles and makes visible settler colonialist logics. Beginning conversations about place with the Indigenous relations of that place exposes settlement as the imposition of logics of ownership and its offshoots such as the commodification of place and people. Grounding understanding of place in the Indigenous relations to that place allows us to more critically see how other stories of place are grafted onto it via places and discourses of public memory.

Offering his perspective on calls to tear the fort down in 2008, historian Bruce White opened his piece with the question, "[w]hat does Fort Snelling say when no one is speaking? The answer to this question is the reason for tearing down the fort."[40] White reflects on the work of his mother, Helen White, whose research in the National Archives in the early 1960s played a part in the fort's reconstruction. Recalling an argument he overheard between his mother and an archeologist who contended that "[i]f I can't see it in the ground it didn't happen," White recalled that his mother did not agree because, as he wrote, "she knew that history was about people's memories and the meanings they invest in places." The stories one sees at the fort are in large part, as White's thoughts reflect, a matter of the perspective brought to bear on the site. The "memories and meanings" that White's mother spoke of are a reflection of one's knowledge and understanding. Yet, the ability to see Indigenous land relations depends on access to the intelligence of which St. John, Waziyatawin, and many others share. Not all intelligences are equally accessible.

The recognition of places like Historic Fort Snelling at Bdote as a Dakota place depends upon a larger, shared, collective knowledge of Dakota as well as the role of the state in systematically undermining Dakota connection to this place. The Bdote Memory Map and Fort Snelling at Bdote invite recognition and re-membering that this is a Dakota place. As such, they are a retort to the logics of settler colonialism as they are imbricated in construction of the original fort and its reconstruction. Events such as the Walker's *Scaffold* exposed the dearth of wider understanding of Dakota history. While the solicitation of Indigenous artists reflects a desire to include Dakota voices and representation, it remains to be seen to what extent this addition will change the underlying logics that led to *Scaffold*. Similarly, The Landing reflects an absence of Indigenous peoples, and the planned innovations reflect a focus on making visible the Dakota relation to the site as well as the wider space. As such, this reflects a focus on making Dakota land relations evident and the role of settler colonialism and its need to continually prop itself up by eschewing Indigenous land relations

This analysis has examined the ways historical places and discourses about them reify particular land relationships and obscure others. History can be used as an attempt to sequester it and its implications from the present. It can also be used to absolve those in the present from acknowledging the past and working for justice in the present. Telling partial histories is a way of expelling the uncomfortable and unresolved tensions of the past. As Anderson and Domosh state, stories of settlement are "national identities that are continually being constructed through narratives of the conquest of Native populations, and the disavowel of that conquest."[41] By consistently telling the story of the Indigenous figure walking into the sunset, and not facing the sunrise, the story of Minnesota is partial and incomplete. Just as it fixes Indigenous figures to the past, it forecloses Indigenous futures. Lt. Governor Flanagan's celebration of the new flag announces Indigenous presence in the present and future. This discussion has implications not only for Indigenous and settler colonial studies, but also for communication studies.

Rethinking Place

Place supersedes and envelopes memory. As communication scholar Greg Dickinson explains, place has horizons of meaning that are known in different ways. Drawing on social theorist Henry Lefebvre and cultural geographer Doreen Massey, Dickinson argues that "space's consequentiality undoes our understanding of linear time." Dickinson thinks about how the past, present, and future are comingled in space. He continues, "the ways in which a place's practice depends on and also remakes memory draws the past into the present and future even as the past it invites is rejiggered."[42] As one engages with a material space, one functions in the present, though does so by taking up remnants of the past, which will be invoked in the future. In that moment and that space, all are equally present. Place is therefore both residual and germinal. It holds horizons of meaning, the raw matter of which is the residuals of the past as they are reworked in the present.

Heretofore, the discussion of place in communication studies is still couched in logics of ownership. Even if we lean into Dickinson's argument, we maintain the premise that place is a thing separate from human/spiritual ontologies. Space, like knowledge in higher education, is something that humans access, acquire, ascertain, package, and exchange for intellectual degrees and/or economic advancement. Communication studies scholar Michael Lechuga argues that the field of rhetorical studies replicates and perpetuates extractivist nodes of settler colonialism. He writes:

> [rhetoric] is a public-facing communication practice that organizes people and materials (especially land) to serve the needs of a settlement through claims of political sovereignty. Furthermore, rhetoric produces and circulates narrative forms that foreclose a postsettler future by reproducing the same sets of relationships between bodies, lands, and power both in our research practices and in our pedagogies.[43]

Rhetorical analysis is extractionist insofar as it extracts, organizes, and packages meaning from/about place. In our studies of place, therefore, rhetoricians commodify those places and the people who hold a relationship with them.[44] In contrast, Lechuga argues for a praxis in which theory is derived from the activist communities and their discourses.

I want to build on Lechuga's argument and go deeper into the idea of theory and praxis emerging from the community from the land. Indigenous studies scholar Coulthard explains place or land. He writes, "[p]lace is a way of knowing, of experiencing and relating to the world and with others; and sometimes these relational practices and forms of knowledge guide forms of resistance against other rationalizations of the world that threaten to erase or destroy our senses of place."[45] This is akin to Indigenous studies scholar Tiara Na'puti, who, using their home as a guiding framework, argues for "oceanic epistemologies" as a counter to rhetoric as a "system of knowledge that has overwhelmingly perpetuated erasure and effacement of Indigenous work."[46] Building on Lechuga, Coulthard, and Na'puti's work, I argue that rhetorical methods brought to bear on a place should emerge from that place and the people who hold a specific relationship with that place insofar as it constitutes their worldview. Research would therefore be relational not only in who or what one examines, but in the epistemologies and methods that informs one's work. Using land as the analytic and seeing research as relational has important implications.

Research becomes a way to recognize and re-source community relations. Methods become known only through communication with communities. This analysis has relied heavily on Indigenous scholarship and, to a significant extent, Dakota scholars and activists. The method of analysis, of breaking down Dakota land relations and seeing how they differ from settler colonialist logics, is derived from the place and people itself. To fully encounter and examine this rhetoric requires doing so with those who themselves are constituted via their land relations. Historian Lorenzo Veracini alludes to this in his argument that writers use "indigenous" and not "Indigenous" because, as Veracini writes, it makes visible that "indigenous peoples retain a better claim than that of settlers because they are indigenous and retain their connection to country/land, not because they are a people; and they are a people because they are sovereign, not because they are indigenous."[47] Much like how Vercini argues that using a lowercase "i" instead of the common uppercase "I" in reference to Indigenous peoples, using land as the guiding analytic calls closer attention to those specific communities whose hold a relationship with specifics lands. It requires a sustained relationship with land and with those who share that relationship. Scholarship then becomes a reflection and reinforcement of that relationship.

With theory emerging from community, and not imposed upon it, rhetorical studies and related fields would proliferate theory as opposed to reanimating neo-Colonialist theory past the point of viability. Understanding refusal as generative entails recognizing that it is ever present and not therefore able to be contained or subsumed under the guise of traditional theory building. Like Lechuga argues, Indigenous theorizing and those who would seek to study

Indigeneity must first understand how Indigenous communities themselves define and practice Indigeneity. Instead of parsimony being a marker of good theory, it would be the antithesis of it. The measure of replicability or universalizing of theory would, and should, render it suspect. This embracing of humility in theorizing, or recognizing the limitations or parameters of applicability of theory, would also make for theory that is much more articulate and reflective of Indigenous land relations.

What does a theory of land as relationship look like? The Maori, the Indigenous peoples of Aotearoa New Zealand, and their work to have their relationships with water recognized illustrate what land-centered epistemology might look like. Originating intellectually with American legal scholar Christopher Stone, who asked if trees should have legal rights, scholars and activists particularly in New Zealand and Australia have had success in arguing for the person-status of waterways. Under the banner of ecological jurisprudence or, as the common Maori saying, "the river is me and I am the river," the being of Maori is directly tied to that of the waterways. This is evident in the testimony of a Palmerston North, Aotearoa, New Zealand community member who is quoted in communication studies scholars Christine Ellas and Mohan Duttas's discussion of how members understand their health as tied to that of the Oroua and other surrounding rivers. The community member stated:

> [t]he glue that held us together [referring to the land] is no longer there and that has created an unwellness and I think that was strategic and the council and governments are, purposefully trying to get more of a stronghold over this land because it is so fertile. And, um, and we are, our rivers are unwell and if we go back to the spiritual being of who we are, they are our veins. So . . . if our veins are unwell, we are unwell. If our land is unwell, we are unwell.

Ellas and Duttas refer to what they argue is needed for community engagement and activism as "voice infrastructures." They explain how land and community conceptualizations of it are central to this work. They write, "[w]e suggest that the turn to land in this sense serves as an anchor for decolonizing health communication through the concept of voice infrastructures, keeping academics in place, situating us in the struggles for land to secure health, locating our bodies in struggles, and holding our bodies accountable."[48] Just as Lechuga argues that rhetorical methods and praxis should emerge from the communities examined themselves, Ellas and Duttas argue that understanding and advocating with and for Indigenous communities requires "the turn to land." Land becomes the means through which subjectivities are constructed rather than those subjectivities being brought to bear on the land.

What is the story of Minnesota as it is told by those who have lived, live, and will live here? It is the land itself; the land holds the stories. It is indeed the farmer settler with the plow, picking rocks, and chopping stumps. It is also, just as much, the Dakota and Anishinaabe and Ho-Chunk. The stories about these places are reified and celebrated via historic sites and the discourses about them. Pulling epistemological fence posts to consider land outside of settler agrarian land logics makes visible not just a deeper understanding and recognition of this place, but of all of its people.

Notes

PREFACE

1. This excerpt begins at 16:00 in a thirty-seven-minute broadcast by Women's Indigenous Media. "Jingle Dress Healing Dance for George Floyd at the Corner of 38th and Chicago Where He Was Murdered in Minneapolis," Women's Indigenous Media Facebook, https://www.facebook.com/watch/live/?ref=watch_permalink&v=601401533915243. A number of mainstream and Indigenous media covered this event. The intersection of Thirty-Eight Street and Chicago Avenue in Minneapolis was officially named George Perry Floyd Square during a ceremony held on the two-year anniversary of Floyd's killing by a Minneapolis police officer. See also "Minneapolis Renames Intersection to Honor George Floyd," *CBS News*, May 26, 2022, https://www.cbsnews.com/news/minneapolis-renames-intersection-to-honor-george-floyd/.
2. Brenda J. Child, *Holding Our World Together: Ojibwe Women and the Survival of Community* (New York: Penguin Books, 2012), 95.
3. According to the April 2022 Minnesota Department of Human Rights study, "Investigation into the City of Minneapolis and the Minneapolis Police Department":

MPD engages in a pattern or practice of discriminatory, race-based policing as evidenced by:

- Racial disparities in how MPD officers use force, stop, search, arrest, and cite people of color, particularly Black individuals, compared to white individuals in similar circumstances.
- MPD officers' use of covert social media to surveil Black individuals and Black organizations, unrelated to criminal activity.
- MPD officers' consistent use of racist, misogynistic, and disrespectful language. (8)

"Investigation in the City of Minneapolis and the Minneapolis Police Department," Minnesota Department of Human Rights, April 27, 2022, https://mn.gov/mdhr/assets/Investigation%20into%20the%20City%20of%20Minneapolis%20and%20the%20Minneapolis%20Police%20Department_tcm1061-526417.pdf.

4. Lenard Monkman, "Jingle Dress Dancers Honour George Floyd at Site Where He Was Killed," Canadian Broadcasting Corporation, June 2, 2020, https://www.cbc.ca/news/indigenous/jingle-dress-dancers-george-floyd-1.5595483.
5. Sheila Regan, "Idle No More Flash Roundy Fills Mall of America Rotunda," *TC Daily Planet*, December 30, 2012, https://www.tcdailyplanet.net/idle-no-more-flash-roundy-mall-america/. See also Andrew Crosby and Jeffrey Monaghan, "Settler Colonialism and the Policing of Idle No More," *Social Justice* 43, no. 2 (2016): 37–57.
6. Leanne Betasamosake Simpson, "Aambe! Maajaadaa! (What #Idlenomore Means to Me)," *Decolonization: Indigeneity, Education and Society*, December 21, 2012. See also Naomi Klein, "Dancing the World into Being: A Conversation with Idle No More's Leanne Simpson," *Yes! Magazine*, March 6, 2013, https://www.yesmagazine.org/social-justice/2013/03/06/dancing-the-world-into-being-a-conversation-with-idle-no-more-leanne-simpson; "A Mall of America Flash Mob for First Nations' Rights," *Yes! Solutions Journalism*, January 5, 2013, https://www.yesmagazine.org/democracy/2013/01/05/mall-of-america-flash-mob-first-nations-rights-idle-no-more; Reyna Crow and Sarah LittleRedfeather, "Idle No More New Year's Eve Round Dance at Mall of America," *Last Real Indians*, December 31, 2013, https://lastrealindians.com/news/2013/12/31/dec-31-2013-for-immediate-release-idle-no-more-new-years-eve-round-dance-at-mall-of-america; Reyna Crow, "Mall of America Threatens Arrest of Idle No More Organizers if New Years Eve Round Dance Occurs—Idle No More," Idle No More, December 25, 2013, https://idlenomore.ca/mall-of-america-threatens-arrest-of-idle-no-more-organizers-if-new-years-eve-round-dance-occurs-idle-no-more/.
7. Patrick Wolfe, "Settler Colonialism and the Elimination of the Native," *Journal of Genocide*

Research 8, no. 4 (2006): 388.

8. A number of research studies document this. See, for example, Matthew Harvey, "Fatal Encounters Between Native Americans and the Police," The Center for Indian Country Development, Minneapolis Federal Reserve, March 2020, https://www.minneapolisfed.org/~/media/assets/articles/2020/fatal-encounters-between-native-americans-and-the-police/fatal-encounters-between-native-americans-and-the-police_march-2020.pdf?la=en and Minnesota Department of Human Rights, "Investigation into the City of Minneapolis and the Minneapolis Police Department," Minnesota Department of Human Rights, April 27, 2022, https://mn.gov/mdhr/assets/Investigation%20into%20the%20City%20of%20Minneapolis%20and%20the%20Minneapolis%20Police%20Department_tcm1061-526417.pdf.
9. Samantha Senda-Cook, Michael K. Middleton, and Danielle Endres, "Interrogating the 'Field,'" in *Text+Field: Innovations in Rhetorical Method*, ed. Sarah L. McKinnon, Robert Asen, Karma R. Chávez, and Robert Glenn Howard (University Park: Pennsylvania State University Press, 2016), 25.
10. Leanne Betasamosake Simpson, *As We Have Always Done: Indigenous Freedom through Radical Resistance* (Minneapolis: University of Minnesota Press, 2020), 176.
11. Aileen Moreton-Robinson, *Critical Indigenous Studies: Engagements in First World Locations* (Tucson: University of Arizona Press, 2016), 5. See also Audra Simpson and Andrea Smith, eds. *Theorizing Native Studies* (Durham: Duke University Press, 2016).
12. Barbie Zelizer explains collective memory as "recollections that are instantiated beyond the individual by and for the collective." Barbie Zelizer, "Reading Against the Grain: The Shape of Memory Studies," *Critical Studies in Mass Communication* 12, no. 2 (1995), 214.
13. Michael Middleton, Aaron Hess, Danielle Endres, and Samantha Senda-Cook, *Participatory Critical Rhetoric: Theoretical and Methodological Foundations for Studying Rhetoric In Situ* (Lanham: Lexington Books, 2015), xiii. See also Greg Dickinson, Carole Blair, and Brian Ott's work on memory places and specifically the ways in which place "exert[s] power through its incorporation, enablement, direction, and constraints on bodies." Carole Blair, Greg Dickinson, and Brian Ott, "Introduction: Rhetoric/Memory/Place," in *Places of Public Memory: The Rhetoric of Museums and Memorials*, ed. Greg Dickinson, Carole Blair, and Brian Ott (Tuscaloosa: University of Alabama Press, 2010), 27. See also Michael K. Middleton, Samantha Senda-Cook, and Danielle Endres, "Articulating Rhetorical Field Methods: Challenges and Tensions," *Western Journal of Communication* 75, no. 4 (2011): 386–406, doi:10.1080/10570314.2011.586969; Carole Blair, "Reflections on Criticism and Bodies: Parables from Public Places," *Western Journal of Communication* 65, no. 3 (2001): 271–294, doi:10.1080/10570310109374706.

14. Audra Simpson, *Mohawk Interruptus: Political Life across the Borders of Settler States* (Durham: Duke University Press, 2014), 35.
15. Tiara R. Na'puti, "Speaking of Indigeneity: Navigating Genealogies against Erasure and #RhetoricSoWhite," *Quarterly Journal of Speech* 105, no. 4 (2010): 495–501.
16. Na'puti, "Speaking of Indigeneity," 498.
17. Romeo García and Damían Baca, eds., *Rhetorics of Elsewhere and Otherwise: Contested Modernities, Decolonial Visions* (Urbana, IL: Conference on College Composition and Communication of the National Teachers of English, 2019), vii.
18. According the Anti-Defamation League, contemporary origin of replacement theory is largely attributed to the French philosopher Renaud Camus who argued that native white Europeans were being replaced by non-white immigrants from central Africa which could lead to the extinction of native whites. Popularized as of late by conservative pundits such as Fox News' Tucker Carlson and others. According to the ADL:

> On April 8, 2021, on *Tucker Carlson Tonight*, the host explicitly promoted the "great replacement" theory. Carlson discussed "Third World" immigrants coming to the U.S. who affiliate with the Democratic Party. He asserted, "I know that the left and all the little gatekeepers on Twitter become literally hysterical if you use the term 'replacement,' if you suggest that the Democratic Party is trying to replace the current electorate—the voters now casting ballots—with new people, more obedient voters from the Third World, but they become hysterical because that's what's happening, actually. Let's just say it. That's true."

Replacement theory is not a one-off or specific to conservative pundits. Politicians, too, have espoused this ideology. According to the ADL, "In March 2017, then-GOP Congressman (IA) Steve King tweeted his support for Geert Wilders, a well-known anti-immigration activist from Europe. Wilders understands that culture and demographics are our destiny," the congressman wrote. "We can't restore our civilization with somebody else's babies." "The Great Replacement: An Explainer," Anti-Defamation League, https://www.adl.org/resources/backgrounders/the-great-replacement-an-explainer.

Finally, replacement theory has been cited by a number of mass murderers in their manifestos. For example, the May 22, 2022, killing of ten people in Buffalo, New York. According to National Public Radio, in his 180-page manifesto, the shooter cited replacement theory and his desire to kill Black people. Emma Bowman, Bill Chapell, Becky Sullivan, "What We Know so Far about the Buffalo Mass Shootings," National Public Radio, May 16, 2022, https://www.npr.org/2022/05/15/1099028397/buffalo-shooting-what-we-know. During the 2017 Charlottesville "Unite the Right" rally, gatherers chanted "you will not replace us." Michael Edison Hayden, Hannah Gais, Cassie Miller, Megan Squire and Jason Wilson, "Unite the Right Five Years Later: Where Are They Now?," Southern Poverty Law Center, August 11, 2022, https://www.splcenter.org/hatewatch/2022/08/11/unite-right-5-years-later-where-are-they-now.

19. Michael Lechuga, *Visions of Invasion: Alien Affects, Cinema, and Citizenship in Settler Colonies* (Jackson: University of Mississippi Press, 2023).
20. Michael Lechuga, "An Anticolonial Future: Reassembling the Way We Do Rhetoric," *Communication and Critical/Cultural Studies* 17, no. 4 (2020): 378, 382.
21. Carole Blair, Greg Dickinson, and Brian Ott, "Introduction: Rhetoric/Memory/Place," in *Places of Public Memory: The Rhetoric of Museums and Memorials*, ed. Greg Dickinson, Carole Blair, and Brian Ott (Tuscaloosa: University of Alabama Press, 2010), 1–54; Carole Blair, Marsha S. Jeppeson, and Enrico Pucci Jr., "Public Memorializing in Postmodernity: The Vietnam Veterans Memorial as Prototype," *Quarterly Journal of Speech* 77 (1991): 263–288; Greg Dickinson, "Memories for Sale: Nostalgia and the Construction of Identity in Old Pasadena," *Quarterly Journal of Speech* 88 (1997): 1–27; Victoria J. Gallagher, "Memory and Reconciliation in the Birmingham Civil Rights Institute," *Rhetoric & Public Affairs* 2, no. 2 (1999): 303–320; Sonja Kuftinec, "[Walking Through a] Ghost Town: Cultural Hauntologie in Mostar, Bosnia-Herzegovina or Mostar: A Performance Review," *Text and Performance Quarterly* 18 (1998): 81–95; J. David Mazon, "'Second in Line to Bury White Supremacy': Take 'Em Down Nola, Monument Removal, and Residual Memory," *Quarterly Journal of Speech* 106, no. 1 (2020): 48–71; Nicholas S. Paliewicz and Marouf Hasian Jr., "Mourning Absences, Melancholic Commemoration, and the Contested Public Memories of the National September 11 Memorial and Museum," *Western Journal of Communication* 80, no. 2 (2016): 140–162; Andrew F. Wood, "Haunting Ruins in a Western Ghost Town: Authentic Violence and Recursive Gaze at Bodie, California," *Western Journal of Communication* 84, no. 4 (2020): 439–456; Elizabethada A. Wright, "Rhetorical Spaces in Memorial Places: The Cemetery as a Rhetorical Memory Place/Space," *Rhetoric Society Quarterly* 35, no. 4 (2005): 51–80.
22. Zelizer, "Reading the Past Against the Grain." See also Jason Black, "Indigenizing the Rhetoric and Public Address Classroom: Memory as a Native American Discursive Tactic," *Communication Teacher* 27, no. 1 (2013): 21–28; Kendall R. Phillips, "The Failure of Memory: Reflections on Rhetoric and Public Remembrance," *Western Journal of Communication* 74, no. 2 (2010): 208–223; Bradford Vivian, "The Art of Forgetting: John W. Draper and the Rhetorical Dimensions of History," *Rhetoric & Public Affairs* 2, no. 4 (1999): 551–572; Bradford Vivian, "Jefferson's Other," *Quarterly Journal of Speech* 88, no. 3 (2002): 284–302.

23. Tamar Katriel, "Sites of Memory: Discourses of the Past in Israeli Pioneering Settlement Museums," *Quarterly Journal of Speech* 80, no. 1 (1994): 3. See also Jason Chalmers, "Settled Memories on Stolen Land: Settler Mythology at Canada's National Holocaust Museum," *American Indian Quarterly* 43, no. 4 (Fall 2019): 379–407.
24. Roger C. Aden, "When Memories and Discourses Collide: The President's House and Places of Public Memory," *Communication Monographs* 79, no. 1 (2012): 72–92; Caitlin Frances Bruce, "Rive of Words as Space for Encounter: Contested Meaning in Rhetorical Convergence Zones," *Quarterly Journal of Speech* 105, no. 4 (2019): 441–464; Chandra Ann Maldonado, "Commemorative (Dis)Placement: On the Limits of Textual Adaptability and the Future of Public Memory Scholarship," *Rhetoric & Public Affairs* 24, no. 1–2 (2021): 239–252; Ryan Erik McGeough, Catherine Helen Palczewski, and Randall A. Lake, "Oppositional Memory Practices as Arguments over Public Memory," *Argumentation and Advocacy* 51 (Spring 2015): 231–254; Mark T. Vail, "Reconstructing the Lost Cause in Memphis City Parks Renaming Controversy," *Western Journal of Communication* 76, no. 4 (2012): 417–437.
25. Greg Dickinson, Brian L. Ott, and Eric Aoki, "Memory and Myth at the Buffalo Bill Museum," *Western Journal of Communication* 69, no. 2 (2005): 85–108; Tricia E. Logan, "Memory, Erasure, and National Myth," in *Colonial Genocide in Indigenous North America*, ed. Andres Woolford, Jeff Benvenuto, and Alexander Laban Hinton (Durham: Duke University Press, 2014), 149–165; Waziyatawin Angela Cavender Wilson, "Burning Down the House: Laura Ingalls Wilder and American Colonialism," in *Unlearning the Language of Conquest: Scholars Expose Anti-Indianism in America*, ed. Four Arrows (Wahinkpe Topa aka Don Trent Jacobs) (Austin: University of Texas Press, 2006), 66–80.
26. Squatters and land speculators were common, as explained by Martin Case. It was common for settlers to settle on land before it had been surveyed and open for sale. Martin Case, *The Relentless Business of Treaties: How Indigenous Land Became U.S. Property* (Saint Paul: Minnesota Historical Society Press, 2018).
27. Mishuana Goeman, "Land as Life: Unsettling the Logics of Containment," *Native Studies Keywords*, ed. Stephanie Nohelani Teves, Andrea Smith, and Michelle H. Raheja (Phoenix: University of Arizona Press, 2015), 74.
28. Vine Deloria Jr., *God Is Red: A Native View of Religion* (Golden: Fulcrum, 2003), xvii.
29. Vine Deloria Jr., *Spirit and Reason: The Vine Deloria Jr. Reader* (Golden: Fulcrum, 1999), 224.
30. Kelsey Marie Carlson, "'We'd Always Return to This Center': Understanding Urban Space as a Dakota Place in Mni Sota Makoce," (master's thesis, Syracuse University, 2015), 28.
31. Gwen Westerman and Bruce White, *Mni Sota Makoce: The Land of the Dakota* (Saint Paul: Minnesota Historical Society Press, 2012), 13.

32. Westerman and White, *Mni Sota Makoce*, 223.
33. Glen S. Coulthard, *Red Skin, White Masks: Rejecting the Colonial Politics of Recognition* (Minneapolis: University of Minnesota Press, 2014), 60, 13.
34. Betasamosake Simpson, *As We Have Always Done*, 43.
35. Betasamosake Simpson, *As We Have Always Done*, 22. See also Leanne Betasamosake Simpson, "Land as Pedagogy: Nishnaabeg Intelligence and Rebellious Transformation," *Decolonization: Indigeneity, Education & Society* 3, no. 3 (2014): 1–25.
36. Goeman, "Land as Life," 79.
37. D. Anthony Tyeeme Clark and Malea Powell, "Resisting Exile in the 'Land of the Free': Indigenous Groundwork at Colonial Intersections," *American Indian Quarterly* 32, no. 1 (2008): 6.
38. Vine Deloria Jr. and Daniel Wildcat, *Power and Place: Indian Education in America* (Golden: Fulcrum, 2001), 13.
39. Deloria., *God Is Red*, 66. See also Vine Deloria Jr., *For This Land: Writings on Religion in America* (New York: Routledge, 1999).
40. Stephen Jay Gould, *Time's Arrow, Time's Cycle: Myth and Metaphor in the Discovery of Geological Time* (Cambridge, MA: Harvard University Press, 1987), 10–11.
41. Johannes Fabian, *Time and the Other: How Anthropology Makes Its Object* (New York: Columbia University Press, 2002), 1. See also Mark Rifkin, *Beyond Settler Time: Temporal Sovereignty and Indigenous Self-Determination* (Durham: Duke University, 2017); Jodi Byrd, *The Transit of Empire: Indigenous Critiques of Colonialism* (Minneapolis: University of Minnesota Press, 2011).
42. Karl Marx, *Capital*, vol. 1 (New York: Vintage, 1973). See also William James Booth, "Economies of Time: On the Idea of Time in Marx's Political Economy," *Political Theory* 19, no. 1 (1991): 7–27.
43. Henri Lefebvre, *The Production of Space*, trans. Donald Nicholson-Smith (Malden, MA: Blackwell, 1984). See also M. Gottdiener, "A Marx for Our Time: Henri Lefebvre and the Production of Space," *Sociological Theory* 11, no. 1 (1983): 129–134.
44. Vine Deloria Jr., *The Metaphysics of Modern Existence* (Colorado Springs: Fulcrum, 2012), 38.
45. Deloria, *God Is Red*, 120–121.
46. Nick Estes, *Our History Is the Future: Standing Rock versus the Dakota Access Pipeline, and the Long Tradition of Indigenous Resistance* (New York: Verso, 2019), 14.
47. Wolfe, "Settler Colonialism and the Elimination of the Native," 388.
48. J. Kēhaulani Kēhaulani Kauanui, "'A Structure, Not an Event': Settler Colonialism and Enduring Indigeneity," *Lateral: A Journal of the Cultural Studies Association* 5, no. 1 (2016), https://csalateral.org/issue/5-1/forum-alt-humanities-settler-colonialism-enduring-

indigeneity-kauanui/.

49. Kēhaulani Kauanui, "A Structure, Not an Event."
50. Tiara Na'puti, "Oceanic Possibilities for Communication Studies," *Communication and Critical/Cultural Studies* 17, no. 1 (2020): 96.
51. Eve Tuck and K. Wayne Yang, "Decolonization Is Not a Metaphor," *Decolonization: Indigeneity, Education & Society* 1, no. 1 (2012): 5, https://jps.library.utoronto.ca/index.php/des/article/view/18630.
52. Tuck and Yang, "Decolonization Is Not a Metaphor," 6.
53. Danielle Endres and Samantha Senda-Cook, "Location Matters: The Rhetoric of Place in Protest," *Quarterly Journal of Speech* 97, no. 3 (2011): 257–282.
54. Frederick Jackson Turner, "The Significance of the Frontier in American History," American Historical Association, Chicago, July 12, 1893. See also Ronald H. Carpenter, "Frederick Jackson Turner and the Rhetorical Impact of the Frontier Thesis," *Quarterly Journal of Speech* 63 (1977): 117–129.
55. Richard Slotkin, *Gunfighter Nation: The Myth of the Frontier in Twentieth-Century America* (Norman: University of Oklahoma Press, 1998), 10. See also, for example, Carpenter, "Frederick Jackson Turner," 117–129.
56. The cultivation of land as a means of establishing property is evident throughout multiple founding philosophical and political texts. John Locke writes in the *Second Treatise*:

    > *As much land* as a Man Tills, Plants, Improves, Cultivates, and can use the Product of, so much is his *Property*. He by his Labour does, as it were, inclose it from the Common . . . God and his Reason commanded him to subdue the Earth, *i.e.* improve it for the benefit of Life, and therein lay out something upon it that was his own, his labour. He that in Obedience to this Command of God, subdued, tilled and sowed parts of it, thereby annexed to it something that was his *Property*, which another had not Title to, nor could without injury take from him.

    John Locke, *Second Treatise on Property* (New York: Blackwell, 1948). The divine edict to "till," "plant," and "cultivate" are the means through which citizens attain property. The argument that God commands that land must be "subdued" is central to what Tully calls Locke's "cultivation argument." James Tully, *A Discourse on Property: John Locke and His Adversaries* (New York: Cambridge University Press, 1980).
57. Michael Schudson, *The Good Citizen: A History of American Civic Life* (Cambridge, MA: Harvard University Press, 1999), 28.
58. Thomas Jefferson, "Notes on Virginia," in *The Life and Selected Writings of Thomas*

Jefferson, ed. Adriene Koch and William Peden (New York: Modern Library, 1944), 280.

59. U.S. Supreme Court, *Johnson v. McIntosh*, February 28, 1823, Justia, https://supreme.justia.com/cases/federal/us/21/543/. See also "Homestead Act," National Archives. The 1866 Fourteenth Amendment guaranteed this to Black men as well. See also "14th Amendment to the U.S. Constitution: Civil Rights (1868)," National Archives, https://www.archives.gov/milestone-documents/14th-amendment. See also "African American Homesteaders in the Great Plains," National Park Service, https://www.nps.gov/articles/african-american-homesteaders-in-the-great-plains.htm.
60. U.S. Supreme Court, *Oliphant vs. Suquamish Indian Tribe*. March 6, 1978, Justia, https://supreme.justia.com/cases/federal/us/435/191/. Robert A. Williams Jr. *Like a Loaded Weapon: The Rehnquist Court, Indian Rights, and the Legal History of Racism in America* (Minneapolis: University of Minnesota Press, 2005), xxii.
61. The Homestead Act made land available to single white men, widows, single women, citizens and immigrants who promised to become citizens. Claimants were required to live on and "improve" the land for five years, upon which time full title would be granted. Claimants could also gain full title after six months, provided they maintained residency, made small improvements, and paid $1.25 an acre. See also "Homestead Act," National Archives, https://www.archives.gov/milestone-documents/homestead-act#:~:text=The%20Homestead%20Act%2C%20enacted%20during,plot%20by%20cultivating%20the%20land.
62. See "Dawes Act," National Archives, https://www.archives.gov/milestone-documents/dawes-act. According to the Indian Land Tenure Foundation, the Dawes Act resulted in the loss of ninety million acres of Native American land and divided tribal communities. "Issues," Indian Land Tenure Foundation, https://iltf.org/land-issues/issues/.
63. This figure is from each of the National Archives' resources on the respective laws.
64. U.S. Supreme Court, *Lyng v. Northwest Indian Cemetery Protective Association*, April 19, 1988, Justia, https://supreme.justia.com/cases/federal/us/485/439/.
65. Robert Nichols, *Theft Is Property: Dispossession & Critical Theory* (Durham: Duke University Press, 2020), 31–32.
66. Patrick Wolfe, "The Settler Complex: An Introduction, Guest Editor," *Settler Colonialism and Native Alternatives in Global Context* 37, no. 2 (2103): 1.
67. Philip J. Deloria, *Playing Indian* (New Haven: Yale University Press, 1998), 187.
68. See, for example, Nicholas Brown and Sarah E. Kanouse, *Re-Collecting Black Hawk: Landscape, Memory, and Power in the American Midwest* (Pittsburgh: University of Pittsburgh Press, 2015).
69. Kevin Bruyneel, "Wake Work Versus Work of Settler Memory: Modes of Solidarity in

#NoDAPL, Black Lives Matter, and Anti-Trumpism," in *Standing with Standing Rock: Voices from the #NoDAPL Movement*, ed. Kevin Bruyneel and Jaskiran Dhillon (Minneapolis: University of Minnesota Press, 2019), 320.

70. Adam J. Barker, "Locating Settler Colonialism," *Journal of Colonialism and Colonial History* 13, no. 3 (2012), https://doi.org/10.1353/cch.2012.0035.
71. Frederick Hoxie, "Retrieving the Red Continent: Settler Colonialism and the History of American Indians in the US," *Ethnic and Racial Studies* 31, no. 6 (2008): 1153–1167.
72. Thomas A. Woods, *Knights of the Plow: Oliver H. Kelley and the Origins of the Grange in Republican Ideology* (Ames: Iowa State University Pres, 1991); Immanuel Ness, "Grange Movement," in *Encyclopedia of American Social Movements* (New York: Routledge, 2004), 777–782; Members of the Sunbeam Grange #2, "State Grange of Minnesota," *MNOpedia*, https://www.mnopedia.org/group/state-grange-minnesota; Immanuel Ness, "Farmer-Labor Party," in *Encyclopedia of American Social Movements* (New York: Routledge, 2004), 818–821; Tom O'Connell, "Minnesota Farmer-Labor Party, 1924–1944," *MNOpedia*, https://www.mnopedia.org/minnesota-farmer-labor-party-1924-1944.
73. In 2020, Minnesota had over 68,000 farms and created over $112 billion in economic activity for the state. Over 450,000 people were employed in agriculture industries. "Economic Analysis and Market Research," Minnesota Department of Agriculture, https://www.mda.state.mn.us/business-dev-loans-grants/economic-analysis-market-research.
74. Dan Gunderson, Elizabeth Dunbar, and Jiwon Choi, "A Look at Minnesota Farming in Seven Charts," *MPR News*, April 11, 2019.
75. See, for example, Casey Ryan Kelly and Jason Edward Black, eds., *Decolonizing Native American Rhetoric: Communicating Self-Determination* (New York: Peter Lang, 2018); and Margret McCue-Enser, "Ada Deer and the Menominee Restoration: Rethinking Native American Protest Rhetoric," *Argumentation* 53, no. 1 (2017): 59–76.
76. Frederick Hoxie, *Talking Back to Civilization: Indian Voices from the Progressive Era* (New York: Bedford, 2001), 5.
77. Glen S. Coulthard, "Subjects of Empire: Indigenous Peoples and the 'Politics of Recognition' in Canada," *Contemporary Political Theory* 6 (2007): 456.
78. Betasamosake Simpson, *As We Have Always Done*, 23, 33.
79. Audra Simpson, "The Ruse of Consent and the Anatomy of 'Refusal': Cases from Indigenous North America and Australia," *Postcolonial Studies* 20, no. 1 (2017): 19.
80. Simpson, *Mohawk Interruptus*, 33, 2–3.
81. Betasamosake Simpson, *As We Have Always Done*, 9.
82. Betasamosake Simpson, *As We Have Always Done*, 49, 176.

83. Simpson, "The Ruse of Consent," 18–33.
84. Simpson, *Mohawk Interruptus*, 11.
85. Simpson, "The Ruse of Consent," 30.
86. Leanne Betasamosake Simpson, *Dancing on Our Turtle's Back: Stories of Nishnaabeg Re-Creation, Resurgence and a New Emergence* (Winnipeg: ARP Books, 2011), 32.
87. Betasamosake Simpson, *As We Have Always Done*, 197.
88. Lorenzo Veracini, "Decolonizing Settler Colonialism: Kill the Settler in Him and Save the Man," *American Indian Culture and Research Journal* 41, no. 1 (2017): 1–18.
89. Jodi A. Byrd, "A Return to the South," *American Quarterly* 66, no. 3 (September 2014): 619.
90. Kim TallBear, "Annual Meeting: The US-Dakota War and Failed Settler Kinship," *Anthropology News* 57, no. 9 (2016): 92–95.
91. Coulthard, *Red Skin, White Masks*, 60.
92. Taiaiake Alfred, "What Is Radical Imagination? Indigenous Struggles in Canada," *Affinities: A Journal of Radical Theory, Culture, and Action* 4, no. 2 (Fall 2010): 5–8.
93. Tiara R. Na'puti and Judy Rohrer, "Pacific Moves Beyond Colonialism: A Conversation from Hawai'i and Guåhan," *Feminist Studies* 43, no. 3 (2017): 537–547.
94. Tiara R. Na'puti, "Oceanic Possibilities for Communication Studies," 95.
95. Audra Simpson, "Whither Settler Colonialism?," *Settler Colonial Studies* 6, no. 4 (2016): 444.
96. Linda Tuhiwai Smith, *Decolonizing Methodologies: Research and Indigenous Peoples*, 2nd ed. (New York: Zed Books, 2012), 2, 5.
97. Darell Enck-Wanzer [Wanzer-Serrano], "Decolonizing Imaginaries: Rethinking 'the People' in the Young Lords' Church Offensive," *Quarterly Journal of Speech* 98, no. 1 (2012): 1–23, https://doi.org/10.1080/00335630.2011.638656; Lisa Flores, "Advancing a Decolonial Rhetoric," *Advances in the History of Rhetoric* 21, no. 3 (2018): 320–322, https://doi.org/10.1080/15362426.2018.1526550; Kent A. Ono, "Darrel Wanzer-Serrano's *The New Young Lords and the Struggle for Liberation*: Theoretical Contributions," *Advances in the History of Rhetoric* 21, no. 3 (2018): 315–319, https://doi.org/10.1080/15362426.2018.1526549; Vincent N. Pham, "Building and Being a Community Control," *Advances in the History of Rhetoric* 21, no. 3 (2018): 323–325, https://doi.org/10.1080/15362426.2018.1531666; Darrell Allan Wanzer [Wanzer-Serrano], "Delinking Rhetoric, or Revisiting McGee's Fragmentation Thesis through Decoloniality," *Rhetoric & Public Affairs* 15, no. 4 (2012): 647–657, https://muse.jhu.edu/article/490122; Darrell Wanzer-Serrano, "Decolonial Rhetoric and a Future Yet-to-Become: A Loving Response," *Advances in the History of Rhetoric* 21, no. 3 (2018): 326–330, https://doi.org/10.1080/15362426.2018.1526551.
98. A number of scholars attend to the question of who can study Native Americans and the questions that should guide non-Native American scholars in such research. See

also Devon Abbott Mihesuah, *So You Want to Write about American Indians? A Guide for Writers, Students, and Scholars* (Lincoln: University of Nebraska Press, 2005); Duane Champagne, "American Indian Studies Is for Everyone," *American Indian Quarterly* 20, no. 1 (1996): 77–82, https://www.jstor.org/stable/1184943.

99. Andrea Smith, "Unsettling the Privilege of Self-Reflexivity," in *Geographies of Privilege*, ed. F. Winndance Twine and B. Gardner (New York: Routledge, 2013), 268.
100. Andrea Smith, "Native Studies at the Horizon of Death: Theorizing Ethnographic Entrapment and Settler Self-Reflexivity," in *Theorizing Native Studies*, ed. Audra Simpson and Andrea Smith (Durham: Duke University Press, 2014), 207–234.
101. Paulette Regan, *Unsettling the Settler Within: Indian Residential Schools, Truth Telling, and Reconciliation in Canada* (Chicago: University of Chicago Press, 2011), 11.

CHAPTER ONE. INDIGENOUS REFUSAL AND REJECTING GENOCIDE

1. When it opened in 1988, the park was celebrated by the *New York Times* as a place for people who would otherwise not enter a museum to encounter art. According to the *Times*, the 12.8-million-dollar project featured forty sculptures on 7.5 acres with Claes Oldenburg and Coosje Van Bruggen's *Spoonbridge and Cherry* as the centerpiece and highlight of the park. "Outdoor Sculptures to Sit on or Climb," *New York Times*, September 4, 1988. The long-celebrated site that is now known as the Minneapolis Sculpture Garden began in 1913 when Minnesota Parks Superintendent Theodore Wirth proposed a garden to be created next door to where the then Armory stood. The Lyndale Park Rose Garden (renamed the Kenwood Gardens) was created in 1907 and, according to the Minneapolis Sculpture Garden website, was the second oldest rose garden in the United States, which was also created by Wirth. The Walker Art Gallery (renamed the Walker Art Center) and the rose garden and stood until 1967 when the construction of federal interstate I-94 destroyed it. In the early 1970s, the Walker Art Center was rebuilt and the Minneapolis Park Board initiated an outdoor art project, *9 Artists, 9 Spaces* in which public art was placed around the city in nine different locations including one next to the Walker. The project quickly failed as many of the sites and art were subject to vandalism. A collaboration between the Walker, which was charged with overseeing the art, and the Minneapolis Park and Recreation Board, which was charged with overseeing the site, led to the opening of the Minneapolis Sculpture Garden in 1988. "History," Minneapolis Park and Recreation Board, https://www.minneapolisparks.org/parks-destinations/

parks-lakes/gardens__bird_sanctuaries/minneapolis_sculpture_garden/#:~:text=The%20history%20of%20the%20Minneapolis,Center%20would%20later%20be%20built.

2. Claes Oldenburg and Coosje van Bruggen, *Spoonbridge and Cherry*, 1988, Walker Sculpture Garden. The *New York Times* describes the piece as "[t]he cherry, [is] nine and a half feet in diameter (the stem is 12 feet long), and a 52-foot-long spoon are made from reinforced aluminum and coated with plastic." "Works in Progress: Pitted Against the Sky," *New York Times*, April 17, 1988. Oldenburg's work is featured at such prestigious galleries as the Tate, the Museum of Modern Art, the Guggenheim, and others. In a December 8, 1994, *CBS News Sunday Morning* episode, "The Oversized Pop Art of Claes Oldenburg," host Charles Osgood states that Oldenburg has completed over twenty-seven large-scale outdoor installations around the world. *CBS Sunday Morning*, aired on December 18, 1994, YouTube, https://www.youtube.com/watch?v=ZrknTntFPdE.
3. Sam Durant, *Scaffold*, Walker Sculpture Garden, 2017. See also Nick Coleman and John Camp, "The Great Dakota Conflict," *St. Paul Pioneer Press Dispatch*, Education Supplement, April 26, 1988; Roxanne Dunbar Ortiz, ed., *The Great Sioux Nation: Sitting in Judgement on America; An Oral History of the Sioux Nation and Its Struggle for Sovereignty* (Lincoln: Bison Books, 2013). Prior to being displayed at the Walker, *Scaffold* was displayed at the Hague in Edinburgh, Scotland, and Kassel, Germany. Described by Sam Durant in his May 29, 2017, public letter:

> This wood and steel sculpture is composite of the representation of seven historical gallows that were used in US state-sanctioned executions by hanging between 1859 and 2006. Of the seven gallows depicted in the work, one in particular recalls the design of the gallows of the execution of the Dakota 38 in Mankato, Minnesota in 1862. . . . Six other scaffolds comprise the sculpture, which include those used to execute abolitionist John Brown (1859); the Lincoln Conspirators (1865), which included the first woman executed in US history; the Haymarket Martyrs (1886), which followed a labor uprising and bombing in Chicago; Rainey Bethea (1936), the last legally conducted public execution in US history; Billy Bailey (1996), the last execution by hanging (not public) in the US; and Saddam Hussein (2006), for war crimes at a joint Iraqi/US facility.

Sam Durant, "A Statement from Sam Durant," Walker Art Center, May 29, 2017, https://walkerart.org/magazine/a-statement-from-sam-durant-05-29-17. In a public letter to *The Circle*, Viso explains how she first encountered Durant's piece and her intention in bringing it to the Walker. She writes: "[W]hen I first encountered *Scaffold* in a sculpture park in Europe five years ago, I saw a potent artistic statement about the ethics of capital punishment. Most importantly, I recognized its capacity to address the buried histories of violence in this country, in particular raising needed awareness among white audiences. I knew this could be a difficult artwork on many levels. This is invariably connected to national issues still embedded in the psyche of this country and its violent, colonialist past." Olga Viso, "Learning in Public: An Open Letter on Sam Durant's *Scaffold*," Walker Art Center, May 26, 2017, https://walkerart.org/magazine/learning-in-public-an-open-letter-on-sam-durants-scaffold.

4. *Dakota 38*, Smooth Feather, 2012, https://www.smoothfeather.com/dakota38; "Watch Dakota 38 Documentary: Remember Those Lost 150 Years Ago," *Indian Country News*, September 13, 2018, https://ictnews.org/archive/watch-dakota-38-documentary-remember-those-lost-150-years-ago.
5. "Dakota 38 Memorial Run," Facebook Group, https://www.facebook.com/groups/237982359700068/; Casey Ek, "Dakota 38 Memorial Run Still Going Strong," *Henderson Independent*, January 1, 2020.
6. Waziyatawin Angela Wilson, ed., *In the Footsteps of our Ancestors: The Dakota Commemorative Marches of the 21st Century* (Saint Paul: Living Justice Press, 2006); "Dakota Commemorative March Retraces 150 Miles of Forced March," *The Circle*, December 16, 2012, https://thecirclenews.org/urban-news/dakota-commemorative-march-retraces-150-miles-of-forced-march/; "Dakota Commemorative March Remembers 1862 Forced March to Fort Snelling," *St. Paul Pioneer Press*, November 11, 2012, https://www.twincities.com/2012/11/11/dakota-commemorative-walk-remembers-1862-forced-march-to-fort-snelling/.
7. Cheyanne St. John, statement given at Walker Art Center, May 31, 2017, published by Lorie Shaull, Walker Art Center, Minneapolis, MN, May 31 2017. Statement confirmed by St. John via email correspondence with author, April 30, 2019. The legal matter of genocide is borne out most succinctly by Waziyatawin in her book *What Does Justice Look Like? The Struggle for Liberation in Dakota Homeland* (Saint Paul: Living Justice Press, 2008). A number of legal scholars examine specific issues central to U.S. and Dakota history and the war. See, for example, Carol Chomsky, "The United States-Dakota War Trials: A Study in Military Injustice," *Stanford Law Review* 43, no. 13 (1990): 13–98; Colette Routel, "Minnesota Bounties on Dakota Men during the U.S.-Dakota War," *William Mitchell Law Review* 40, no. 1 (2013): 1–77; and Howard J. Vogel, "Rethinking the Effect of the Abrogation of the Dakota Treaties and the Authority for the Removal of the Dakota People from Their Homeland," *William Mitchell Law Review* 39, no. 2 (2013): 538–581.
8. After his death (1863) Taoyateduta's body was repeatedly desecrated, ultimately his scalp

and one of his forearm bones was displayed at the Minnesota State Capital until 1918 when a grandson of Taoyateduta saw it and asked that it be removed. For fifty years it sat in storage until 1971 when a Minnesota State Historical Society member returned it to Flandreau, South Dakota, where it is buried. See Curt Brown, "Little Crow's Legacy," *Star Tribune* (Minneapolis), August 17, 2012.

9. Ashley Fairbanks, "Genocide and Mini-Golf in the Walker Sculpture Garden," *City Pages*, May 27, 2017.
10. My reference to the Minnesota River Valley reflects a reference common in Minnesota both to the geographical area surrounding the Minnesota River as well as a socio-cultural reference. There is, for example, the Minnesota River Valley Scenic Byway, which is promoted by the Upper Minnesota River Valley, *Explore Minnesota*, and "America's Byways," which is an arm of the U.S. Department of Transportation. According to the USDOT, "America's Byways":

    > is the umbrella term we use for the collection of 150 distinct and diverse roads designated by the U.S. Secretary of Transportation. America's Byways include the National Scenic Byways and All-American Roads. America's Byways are gateways to adventures where no two experiences are the same.
    >
    > The National Scenic Byways Program invites you to Come Closer to America's heart and soul.

    "America's Byways," U.S. Department of Transportation: Federal Highway Administration, https://www.fhwa.dot.gov/byways/.
11. Since the first land surveys in the 1880s, extensive burial mounds have been documented throughout the area. "Concept Master Plan: Historic Murphy's Landing," Shakopee City Council, Meeting Agenda, Packet General Meeting, General Business, January 25, 2007, https://forms.shakopeemn.gov/WebLink/DocView.aspx?id=101960&dbid=0&repo=Shakopee.

    According to the *Shakopee Valley News*, July 29, 1987, the Scott County Historical Society received a quitclaim deed from the city for eighty-seven acres of property in the early 1970s and an additional eleven acres in 1977. The historical society then created the Minnesota Valley Restoration Project and set up a board to run Murphy's Landing. Patrick Minelli, "Council Seeks Options on Issues of Management at Murphy's Landing," *Shakopee Valley News*, July 29, 1987, 1.

    In 1972, the Minnesota Valley Restoration Project (MVRP) secured registry National Register of Historic Places for the Shakopee Historic District, which included The Landing. National Register of Historic Places Inventory Nomination Form, "Shakopee

Historic District," U.S. Department of the Interior, April 11, 1972.

The site became a focus of contention in 1987 when the city of Shakopee sought to take ownership of The Landing back from the Scott County Historical Society and the MVRP over claims of mismanagement. In 2002, the MVRP was dissolved and the Three Rivers Park District took over the site. The site was owned by the city of Shakopee. It was at this time that plans to revitalize the site started to take shape. Tim Harlow, "History Will Live on at Murphy's Landing: Three Rivers Park District Has Taken Over the Shakopee Attraction," *Star Tribune* (Minneapolis), May 8, 2002, 1B; Tim Harlow, "Rising from the Ashes: In the Wake of an Off-Season Fire, Volunteers Will Keep Living History Going at Murphy's Landing," *Star Tribune* (Minneapolis), May 25, 2001; David Peterson, "A New Mission for the Landing," *Star Tribune* (Minneapolis), July 5, 2008.

12. "Murphy's Inn," The Landing: Minnesota River Heritage Park, *Three Rivers Park District*. The entire sign reads:

> Murphy's Inn
> The foundation before you is all that remains of the stone house and inn built by Richard G. Murphy around 1858. At that time, this property was situated at the crossroads of major river and stagecoach transportation routes. In its heyday, Murphy's Inn was likely a welcome site to weary travelers journeying up the Minnesota River Valley. A large main hall on the first floor provided guests with food and drink, while rooms on the second floor could be rented for overnight lodging.
>
> Who was Richard Murphy?
> Richard Murphy first arrived at Fort Snelling in 1848 as President James K. Polk's appointed Indian Agent to the Dakota Nation. He was heavily involved in politics throughout his life, having served for 12 years in the Illinois legislature before moving to Minnesota. In 1857, Murphy was elected to the Minnesota territorial legislature as Senator from Shakopee. He was president of the senate in 1858 when Minnesota voted for statehood. Richard Murphy died in 1875.

13. "Medicine Bottle," The U.S.-Dakota War of 1862, Minnesota Historical Society, http://www.usdakotawar.org/history/multimedia/medicine-bottle. There are many places to access this information, including but not limited to, "Our History," Shakopee Mdewakanton Sioux Community, https://shakopeedakota.org/culture/our-native-american-history and Westerman and White, who write:

> The Bdewakaŋtuŋwaŋ village located farthest upstream on the Minnesota River and the one with the largest population in the mid-nineteenth century was Ṡakṗe's village, or village of the Six, located in various places new present-day Shakopee. The Dakota name was Tiŋta Otoŋwe, meaning "village of the prairie," a reference to the unwooded land on the terrace on the river's south side. In 1823 the village was located on the north side of the river, where cornfields and burial scaffolds were found, although explorer Stephen Long may have confused scaffolds for drying corn with those used for burial. At that time a cemetery and a cornfield were also located on the south side of the river. Taliaferro called the village "twenty mile village." Its leader bore the hereditary name Ṡakṗe, the Six (though with one generation it was Ṡakpedaŋ, Little Six).

Westerman and White, *Mni Sota Makoce*, 125.

14. The reference 38+2, used during the *Scaffold* protest and in other Dakota references to the war, refers to the 38 Dakota hanged in Mankato as well as Ṡakṗe and Wa-kan-o-zhan zhan. In LeMay's May 30, 2017, *Indian Country Today* piece "Peaceful Protests Continue at the Site, where the Partially Erected 'Scaffold' can be Seen." A website, Not Art 38+2, and a social media condemnation at #Takeitdown also contributed to the art center's rethinking of the installation. Konnie LeMay, "*Scaffold* Sculpture Taints Memory of Dakota 38, Prompts Protests," *Indian Country Today*, May 30, 2017, https://ictnews.org/archive/scaffold-sculpture-taints-memory-dakota-38-prompts-protests. Writing about what Fort Snelling means to Sheldon Wolfchild, descendant of Medicine Bottle, LeMay writes, "the fort holds particular pain because it is where his ancestor, Medicine Bottle, was hanged along with Little Six; they are the two killed after the mass execution and remembered as the Dakota 38+2." Konnie LeMay, "Dakota Elders Will Oversee Dismantling, Burning of 'Scaffold,' *Indian Country Today*, June 1, 2017, https://newsmaven.io/indiancountrytoday/archive/dakota-elders-will-oversee-dismantling-burning-of-scaffold-19_sDGCaf0O1hDGe0q80Wg.
15. The city of Mankato's website describes the park, dedicated in 1997, as "a site to reflect, meditate and remember." See "Dakota Monuments: Reconciliation Park," Visit Greater Mankato, https://www.visitgreatermankato.com/mankato/explore/history/dakota-monuments/.
16. While many examples of this abound, the use of Indigenous figures as mascots is particularly reflective of putting representations of Indigenous peoples in service to narratives of colonialism. See, for example, Danielle Endres, "American Indian Permission for Mascots: Resistance or Complicity Within Rhetorical Colonialism?," *Rhetoric & Public Affairs* 18, no. 4: 649–690.

17. J. Kēhaulani Kauanui, "'A Structure, Not and Event': Settler Colonialism and Enduring Indigeneity," *Lateral: A Journal of Cultural Studies* 5, no. 1 (2016), https://csalateral.org/issue/5-1/forum-alt-humanities-settler-colonialism-enduring-indigeneity-kauanui/.
18. *The Landing Journal: Murphy's Landing, a Minnesota Valley Restoration of 1840–1890*, Gale Family Library, Minnesota Historical Society, spring 1990.
19. Oliver Faribault alone is representative of the complexity of the time and the people. His cabin was moved from across Highway 101 to The Landing where on the brochures and the *Landing Journal* he is known simply as the "fur trader." Faribault's mother was a Dakota French woman named Pelagie Kinie Ainsse (or Hanse) and Faribault married a Dakota French woman named Henriette Manegie. The cabin is said to be the first home built in Scott county, Minnesota. "The Faribault Cabin," *Landing Journal*, spring 1990, Minnesota Historical Society Gale Family Research Library. These treaties resulted in the sale of almost all Dakota land; after signing them, Dakota were relegated to a twenty-mile strip of land on either side of the Minnesota River. See "Relations: Dakota and Ojibwe Treaties," TreatiesMatter.org, http://treatiesmatter.org/treaties/land/1837-ojibwe-dakota.
20. "The Landing," brochure, Three Rivers Park District.
21. "The Landing," Three Rivers Park District, https://www.threeriversparks.org/location/landing.
22. "Summer Camps," Three Rivers Park District, https://www.threeriversparks.org.
23. See, for example, Angela Cavender Wilson, "Burning Down the House: Laura Ingalls Wilder and American Colonialism," in *Unlearning the Language of Conquest*, ed. Donald Jacobs (Austin: University of Texas Press, 2006), 65–80.
24. Jodi Byrd, *The Transit of Empire: Indigenous Critiques of Colonialism* (Minneapolis: University of Minnesota Press, 2011), xx.
25. According to *Minnesota River Terminals*, Ports and Waterways Section, CHS Terminal in Savage has a capacity of 560,000 bushels. Minnesota Department of Transportation, *Minnesota River Terminals*, 2013:40.
26. According to the 2018 Shakopee Mdewakanton Sioux Community Donation Report, "In fiscal year 2018 alone, we provided $18 million in donations for education, youth programming, health care programs, legal aid, community development and infrastructure, women's health, arts and culture, local communities, environmental protection, and many more worthwhile causes and enterprises." Shakopee Mdewakanton Sioux Community, *2018 Donation Report: Shakopee Mdewakanton Sioux Community* (Prior Lake, MN: Shakopee Mdewakanton Sioux Community, April 15, 2019) https://shakopeedakota.org/resources/smsc-reports-links.
27. Waziyatawin, "The Paradox of Indigenous Resurgence at the End of Empire,"

Decolonization: Indigeneity, Education & Society 1, no. 72 (2012): 68–85, 72, https://jps.library.utoronto.ca/index.php/des/article/view/18629.

28. Corey Snelgrove, Rita Kaur Dhamoon, and Jeff Corntassel, "Unsettling Settler Colonialism: The Discourse and Politics of Settlers, and Solidarity with Indigenous Nations," *Decolonization: Indigeneity, Education& Society* 3, no. 2 (2014): 4–5.
29. Kay Anderson and Mona Domosh, "North American Spaces/Postcolonial Stories," *Cultural Geographies* 9 (2002): 125–126.
30. David Peterson, "A New Mission for the Landing," *Star Tribune* (Minneapolis), July 5, 2008.
31. Sam Durant, "A Statement from Sam Durant," *Walker Art Magazine*, May 29, 2017, https://walkerart.org/magazine/a-statement-from-sam-durant-05-29-17.
32. Kay Anderson and Mona Domosh, "North American Spaces/Postcolonial Stories," *Cultural Geographies* 9 (2002): 126.
33. Coulthard, "Subjects of Empire," 49.
34. Viso, "Learning in Public: An Open Letter on Sam Durant's Scaffold."
35. LeMay, "*Scaffold* Sculpture."
36. Audra Simpson, "The Ruse of Consent and the Anatomy of 'Refusal': Cases from Indigenous North America and Australia," *Postcolonial Studies* 20, no. 1 (2017): 22.
37. Glen S. Coulthard, "Subjects of Empire: Indigenous Peoples and the 'Politics of Recognition' in Canada," *Contemporary Political Theory* 6 (2007): 453.
38. Chester M. Oehler, *The Great Sioux Uprising* (New York: Oxford University, 1997). See also Duane P. Schultz, *Over the Earth I Come: The Great Sioux Uprising of 1862* (New York: St. Martin's Press, 1993). Schultz had the honor of writing a 1992 *New York Times* Notable Book of the Year. Finally, see Kenneth Carley, *The Sioux Uprising of 1862* (Saint Paul: Minnesota Historical Society Press, 1976), retitled *The Dakota War of 1862: Minnesota's Other Civil War* in 2001. The change in titles of Carley's work reflects the change in general understanding of the war.
39. Simpson, *Mohawk Interruptus*, 33.
40. "Dakota Elders Announcement," All My Relations Arts, May 29, 2017, http://www.allmyrelationsarts.com/dakota-elders-announcement/
41. Alicia Eler, "2017 Moments: 'Scaffold' Ignited a Debate about Art and Cultural Appropriation," *Star Tribune* (Minneapolis), December, 28, 2017, http://www.startribune.com/2017-moments-scaffold-ignited-a-debate-about-art-and-cultural-appropriation/467032633/.
42. This quote, or amalgamations of it, are attributed to Trudell in multiple places. For example, it is available here in the speech transcript of a commemoration he gave for Judi Bari in 1997: http://sisis.nativeweb.org/sov/trudbari.html. And, while it is attributed

to him, it is used by groups and people such as here: https://www.facebook.com/nativelivesmatter1/posts/our-intelligence-is-the-antibiotic/1899408096760786/.

43. Leanne Betasamosake Simpson, *As We Have Always Done: Indigenous Freedom through Radical Resistance* (Minneapolis: University of Minnesota Press, 2020), 185.
44. Leanne Betasamosake Simpson, *Dancing on Our Turtle's Back: Stories of Nishnaabeg Re-Creation, Resurgence and a New Emergence* (Winnipeg: ARP Books, 2011), 24.
45. Jenna Ross, "At Walker, American Indian Artists Discuss the Art World: 'These Changes need to be Permanent,'" *Star Tribune* (Minneapolis), March 30, 2018.
46. "Indigenous Arts Commission: Call to Artists," Walker Art Center, https://walkerart.org/call-to-artists-indigenous-public-art-commission.
47. "Walker Art Center Announces Artist Angela Two Stars as Finalist for Indigenous Public Art Commission in the Minneapolis Sculpture Garden," Walker Art Center, September 17, 2019, https://walkerart.org/press-releases/2019/walker-art-center-announces-artist-angela-two-stars-as-finalist-for-indigenous-public-art-commission-in-the-minneapolis-sculpture-garden.
48. Angela Two Stars, "Okciyapi," *Walker Art Museum Magazine*, https://walkerart.org/magazine/okciyapi-angela-two-stars.
49. Mason Riddle, "Ripple Effects: A Conversation with Angela Two Stars," *Sculpture: A Publication of the International Sculpture Center*, August 11, 2022, https://sculpturemagazine.art/ripple-effects-a-conversation-with-angela-two-stars/.
50. *Shakopee Riverfront Cultural Trail: Visitor Experience Plan* (Saint Paul: 106 Group, May 28, 2021), 12, 16, https://shakopee.org/wp-content/uploads/2021/07/SRCT-Final-VEP-2021-05-28_reduced.pdf.
51. *Shakopee Riverfront Cultural Trail.*
52. *Shakopee Riverfront Cultural Trail.*
53. *Shakopee Riverfront Cultural Trail.*

CHAPTER TWO. REPARATIVE JUSTICE AND INTERVENTIONS IN SETTLER NOSTALGIA

1. John Stoesz, "Written Support of S.F. 1087," Minnesota State Senate, https://www.senate.mn/committees/2021-2022/3112_Committee_on_Labor_and_Industry_Policy/John%20Stoesz.Written%20support%20of%20SF1087.pdf. Ashley Stewart, "Minnesota Native Bicycles to Promote Dakota Land," *Blooming Prairie Leader* (Blooming Prairie, MN), October 18, 2013.

2. Edie Schmierbach, "Cyclist Promotes Land Recovery for Dakota," *Free Press* (Mankato, MN), October 13, 2013.
3. "Our Dream," Makoce Ikikcupi: A Project of Reparative Justice, https:makoceikikcupi.com.
4. Leanne Betasomasake Simpson, "Indigenous Resurgence and Co-Resistance," *Critical Ethnic Studies* 2, no. 2. (2016): 23.
5. Schmeirbach, "Cyclist Promotes Land Recovery for Dakota."
6. Leanne Betasamosake Simpson, *Dancing on Our Turtle's Back: Stories of Nishnaabeg Re-Creation, Resurgence and a New Emergence* (Winnipeg: ARP Books, 2011), 17–18.
7. Minnesota Century Farm Recognition Program Application, Minnesota Farm Bureau, fbmn.org.
8. Minnesota Century Farm Recognition Program, Minnesota Farm Bureau.
9. "Farm Bureau Recognizes Sesquicentennial Farms," *Winona Post* (MN), April 15, 2020.
10. Dan Browing, "Minnesota's 'Century Farms' Total Nearly 11,000," *Star Tribune* (Minneapolis).
11. Browing, "Minnesota's 'Century Farms' Total Nearly 11,000."
12. "History: Timeline," Minnesota State Fair, https://www.mnstatefair.org/general-info/history-timeline/.
13. Noelani Goodyear-Ka'ōpua, *The Seeds We Planted: Portraits of a Native Hawaiian Charter School* (Minneapolis: University of Minnesota Press, 2020), 30, 36.
14. Eve Tuck and K. Wayne Yang, "Decolonization Is Not a Metaphor," *Decolonization: Indigeneity, Education & Society* 1, no. 1 (2012): 5, https://jps.library.utoronto.ca/index.php/des/article/view/18630.
15. Godfried Agyeman Asante, "#RhetoricSoWhite and US Centered: Reflections on Challenges and Opportunities," *Quarterly Journal of Speech* 104, no. 4 (2019): 487.
16. Harsha Walia, "Moving beyond a Politics of Solidarity towards a Practice of Decolonization," Colours of Resistance Archive, http://www.coloursofresistance.org/769/moving-beyond-a-politics-of-solidarity-towards-a-practice-of-decolonization/.
17. Corey Snelgrove, Rita Kaur Dhamoon, and Jeff Corntassel, "Unsettling Settler Colonialism: The Discourse and Politics of Settlers, and Solidarity with Indigenous Nations," *Decolonization: Indigeneity, Education& Society* 3, no. 2 (2014): 27, https://jps.library.utoronto.ca/index.php/des/article/view/21166.
18. Tiara R. Na'puti, "Speaking of Indigeneity: Navigating Genealogies against Erasure and #RhetoricSoWhite," *Quarterly Journal of Speech* 105, no. 4 (2010): 496.
19. Glen Coulthard and Leanne Betasamosake Simpson, "Grounded Normativity and Place-Based Solidarity," *American Quarterly* 68, no. 2 (2016): 249–255.

20. Tiara Na'puti, "Oceanic Possibilities for Communication Studies," *Communication and Critical/Cultural Studies* 17, no. 1 (2020): 96.
21. Vine Deloria Jr. and Daniel Wildcat, *Power and Place: Indian Education in America* (Golden: Fulcrum, 2001), 27.
22. Betasamosake Simpson, *As We Have Always Done*, 43.
23. Glen Coulthard, "From Wards of the State to Subjects of Recognition? Marx, Indigenous Peoples, and the Politics of Dispossession in Denendeh," in *Theorizing Native Studies*, ed. Audra Simpson and Andrea Smith (Durham: Duke University Press, 2014), 62.
24. Noelani Goodyear-Ka'ōpua, *The Seeds We Planted: Portraits of a Native Hawaiian Charter School* (Minneapolis: University of Minnesota Press, 2013), 30, 36.
25. Gwen Westerman and Bruce White, *Mni Sota Makoce: The Land of the Dakota* (Saint Paul: Minnesota Historical Society Press, 2012), 13.
26. Katherine E. Beane, "Woyakapi Kin Ahdipi "Bringing the Story Home": A History Within the Wakpa Ipaksan Dakota Oyate" (doctoral dissertation, University of Minnesota, November 2014), 223.
27. Avery Jones, "Name Restoration," Bda Maka Ska, https://bdemakaska.net/place/name-restoration/. Bde Maka Ska is a lake which received great attention after the Minnesota Department of Natural Resources changed it from Lake Calhoun. A challenge by the Minneapolis Park Board over the rights of the MN DNR to change was lost in court on May 13, 2020. See Aliyah Chavez, "History Restored: Family Celebrates Return of Bde Maka Ska Lake Name," *Indian Country Today*, May 14, 2020, https://indiancountrytoday.com/news/history-restored-family-celebrates-return-of-bde-maka-ska-lake-name-zIUe198vhk6KnW1icY8SYw.
28. Andrea Smith, "Indigeneity, Settler Colonialism, White Supremacy," in *Racial Formation in the Twenty-First Century*, ed. Daniel Martinez, Ho Sang, and Laura Pulido (Berkeley: University of California Press, 2012).
29. Terri Washburn, "One Hundred and Fifty Years of Farming for Sands Family," *Kenyon Leader* (MN), June 21, 2013.
30. Lisa Phillips, "Wright County Sisters Feted for Their 150-Year-Old Farm," *Delano Eagle* (MN), October 17, 2008.
31. As with any historical conflict, there is much to the U.S.-Dakota war. Briefly, the war resulted in the largest mass execution by the U.S. government when on December 26, 1862, 38 Dakota men were hanged. Sixteen hundred Dakota women, children, and elderly were marched to Fort Snelling in Saint Paul, Minnesota, where over the course of the winter, over three hundred died. Dakota men were interned at Camp McClellen. See "Forced Marches and Imprisonment," U.S.-Dakota War, Minnesota Historical Society,

https://www.usdakotawar.org/history/aftermath/forced-marches-imprisonment.

32. Smith, "Indigeneity, Settler Colonialism, White Supremacy."
33. Jodi Byrd, *The Transit of Empire: Indigenous Critiques of Colonialism* (Minneapolis: University of Minnesota Press, 2011), xx.
34. Kay Anderson and Mona Domosh, "North American Spaces/Postcolonial Stories," *Cultural Geographies* 9 (2002): 125.
35. July Lawhon, "Celebrating One Farm, One Family, 100 Years," *White Bear Lake Press* (MN).
36. Washburn, "One Hundred and Fifty Years of Farming for Sands Family."
37. Tuck and Yang, "Decolonization Is Not a Metaphor," 6–7.
38. Ryan Anderson, "Century Farm: Krause Family Honored as Century Farm," *Faribault Daily News*, October 12, 2018.
39. While the economic pressures facing independent farmers reaches back to the 1970s, recently things have deteriorated. According to University of Minnesota Extension data published by the *Star Tribune*, "Median income for Minnesota farmers in 2018 was already at a 23-year low, and 34% of farming operations lost money." The article continues, "[m]eanwhile debt held by American farmers has risen to levels last seen in the 1980s, Agriculture Secretary Sonny Perdue told a congressional committee in February." "Rain on the Scarecrow, Again," *Star Tribune* (Minneapolis), May 16, 2019.
40. Lauren Kotajarvi, "Sesquicentennial Farm Carries on for Six Generations," *Post-Bulletin*, June 20, 2016.
41. Howard J. Vogel, "The Clash of Stories at Chimney Rock: A Narrative Approach to Cultural Conflict over Native American Sacred Sites on Public Land," *Santa Clara Law Review* 41, no. 3 (2001): 760–761. For more on the Chimney Rock case, see U.S. Reports: Lyng v. Northwest Indian Cemetery Prot. Assn., 485 U.S. 439 (1988).
42. Robert Nichols, *Theft Is Property: Dispossession & Critical Theory* (Durham: Duke University Press, 2020), 31–32.
43. Audra Simpson, *Mohawk Interruptus: Political Life across the Borders of Settler States* (Durham: Duke University Press, 2014), 22.
44. Simpson, *Mohawk Interruptus*, 11.
45. Glen S. Coulthard, *Red Skin, White Masks: Rejecting the Colonial Politics of Recognition* (Minneapolis: University of Minnesota Press, 2014), 18.
46. See Valerie N. Wieskamp and Cortney Smith, "'What to Do When You're raped': Indigenous women critiquing and coping through a rhetoric of survivance," *Quarterly Journal of Speech* 20, no. 1: 72–94.
47. "Our Dream," Makoce Ikikcupi (Land Recovery): A Project of Reparative Justice, https://makoceikikcupi.com/our-dream/.

48. "Our First Village," Makoce Ikikcupi (Land Recovery): A Project of Reparative Justice, https://makoceikikcupi.com/our-first-village.
49. "Our Dream."
50. Leanne Betasamosake Simpson, *As We Have Always Done: Indigenous Freedom through Radical Resistance* (Minneapolis: University of Minnesota Press, 2020), 43.
51. "Our Dream."
52. Goodyear-Ka'ōpua, *The Seeds We Planted*, xvi.
53. Schmierbach, "Cyclist Promotes Land Recovery for Dakota."
54. Coulthard, "From Wards of the State to Subjects of Recognition?," 62.
55. "Our Dream."
56. According to its website, the mission of Dream of Wild Health is "to restore health and well-being in the Native community by recovering knowledge of and access to healthy Indigenous foods, medicines and lifeways." Originally called Peta Wakan Tipi, the nonprofit was established in 1986 as a housing and culturally based treatment program. In 1998, the organization transitioned and was renamed Dream of Wild Health. Currently, the program offers Indigenous food tastings and youth gardening programs. https://dreamofwildhealth.org/.
57. Diane Wilson, *Beloved Child: A Dakota Way of Life* (Saint Paul: Minnesota Historical Society, 2011), 8.
58. Westerman and White, *Mni Sota Makoce*, 13.
59. Anne Kopas, "Jacobson Farm a Marker of Dairy Life in Decades Gone By," *Faribault Daily News*, October 3, 2019.
60. Howard J. Vogel, "Healing the Trauma of America's Past: Restorative Justice, Honest Patriotism, and the Legacy of Ethnic Cleansing," *Buffalo Law Journal* 55, no. 3 (2007): 1006.
61. Paulette Regan, *Unsettling the Settler Within: Indian Residential Schools, Truth Telling, and Reconciliation in Canada* (Chicago: University of Chicago Press, 2011), 11.
62. "Our Dream."
63. Schmierbach, "Cyclist Promotes Land Recovery for Dakota."
64. "Our First Village."

CHAPTER THREE. DAKOTA MEMORY MAPS AND RE-MEMBERING THE LAND

1. "What Is Bdote?," Bdote Memory Map, http://bdotememorymap.org/memory-map/#.
2. As the online Memory Map is always accessible, and the tour is accessible through

scheduled events coordinate by the Minnesota Humanities Center, I focus analysis here on the website.

3. "About This Site," Makoce Ikikcupi, https://bdotememorymap.org/memory-map.
4. Little Earth, "Little Earth: A Community Blooming Where we are Planted." Little Earth Housing Complex is the first urban Indigenous-exclusive Section 8 housing complex in the country. According to the website, "Little Earth is a 9.4 acre, 212-unit Housing and Urban Development (HUD) subsidized housing complex located in the urban industrial core of Minneapolis, Minnesota. Little Earth was founded in 1973 and remains the only indigenous preference project-based Section 8 rental assistance community in the United States." Little Earth, https://www.littleearth.org/. Minneapolis American Indian Center, founded in 1975, provides cultural resources and services to the local and wider Indigenous community. Minneapolis American Indian Center, https://www.maicnet.org/. The area of Franklin Avenue, where All My Relations Gallery is located, has been a center of urban Indigenous people and culture since the 1970s when the American Indian Movement was founded nearby. Today, it is the center of Indigenous culture and development. According to The American Indian Cultural Corridor:

> The American Indian Cultural Corridor's name and conceptual identity is the work of the Minneapolis-based Native American Community Development Institute.
>
> The goal is to re-brand the traditional heart of the city's Native American community as a place where both Indians and tourists can enjoy Native American food, art, and culture on Franklin Avenue and in the Phillips Neighborhood of Minneapolis, Minnesota.
>
> Minneapolis, Minnesota is home to one of the largest concentrations of urban Native Americans in the U.S. For the last forty years, Franklin Avenue in south Minneapolis has been the heart of this community: a place where American Indians live, work, and access cultural-specific services. Today, this presence is visible in the various American Indian institutions clustered on and around the avenue, including urban tribal offices, the American Indian Center, All My Relations Arts Gallery, Little Earth Housing Corporation, the American Indian Industrial Opportunities Center, and the Indian Health Board.

"About the Corridor," American Indian Community Cultural Corridor, https://www.nacdi.org/cultural-corridor. See also Laura Waterman Wittstock and Dick Bancroft, *We Are Still Here: A Photographic History of the American Indian Movement* (Saint Paul: Minnesota Historical Society Press, 2013), 3–7.

5. The Indian Relocation Act, 1953, P.L. 959. See also Mato Canali Winyan, "Part One: The Indian Relocation Act," *Lakota Times*, October 26, 2022, https://www.lakotatimes.com/articles/part-1-indian-relocation-act/; Mato Canali Winyan, "Li'la Wota'ku'ye Ota'pi," *Lakota Times*, February 8, 2023, https://www.lakotatimes.com/articles/lila-wotakuye-otapi/, May 22, 2023; Max Nesterack, "Uprooted: The 1950s Plan to Erase Indian Country," *MPR News*, November 4, 2019, https://www.mprnews.org/story/2019/11/04/uprooted-the-1950s-plan-to-erase-indian-country; Gloria Hillard, "Urban American Indians Rewrite Relocation's Legacy," National Public Radio, January 7, 2012, https://www.npr.org/2012/01/07/143800287/urban-american-indians-rewrite-relocations-legacy.
6. "About This Site."
7. Mariane Combs, "'City Indians' Use Art to Stake Their Claim," *MPR News*, November 15, 2006, https://www.mprnews.org/story/2006/11/15/cityindians.
8. "Two Minneapolis Police Officers Were Guilty of Racial Discrimination When They Put Two Drunken Indians in the Trunk of Their Patrol Car for a Trip to the Hospital, a State Agency Ruled Thursday," AP News, https://apnews.com/article/4a387bd09f8cb274ca0cc6d02fefae74; See also "Shielded from Justice: Police Accountability in the United States," Human Rights Watch, https://www.hrw.org/legacy/reports98/police/uspo86.htm#P2346_595050. Smith was not the only Indigenous artist to use their work as a form of talking back. Artist Jim Denomie's *Attack on Fort Snelling Bar and Grill* includes a reference to the Minneapolis police incident as well. The *Weisman Art Museum News*, September 1, 2012, describes his work and this painting. Reporters Maple and O'Brien write:

    > [i]n the scholarly field of art history, iconography is the practice of identifying and interpreting symbols, icons, and the content of imagery in a work of art. Jim Denomie describes his painting *Attack on Fort Snelling Bar and Grill* as "a visual story about some of the historical events concerning the state of Minnesota and the Ojibwe and Dakota tribes within its boundaries since the 1862 Dakota War." A native of the Midwest and a member of the Lac Courte Oreilles Band of Ojibwe, Denomie paints stories from his own dreams and experiences, as well as historical events, including many that have been harmful and hurtful to the American Indian community. Often these scenes express sarcasm or anger at the attitudes developed during these events. . . .
    >
    > Further down the left side, a Native American and a horse are in the trunk of a police car. This refers to an incident in April 1993 when two Minneapolis

officers were suspended for taking two intoxicated Native Americans to the hospital in the trunk of their car.

Emily Maple, E. Gerald, and Lisa O'Brien, "Focus on the Collection—Decoding Jim Denomie's Attack on Fort Snelling Bar and Grill," *Weisman Art Museum News*, September 1, 2012, https://wam.umn.edu/2012/09/01/focus-on-the-collection-decoding-jim-denomies-attack-on-fort-snelling-bar-and-grill/.

9. "Update on Police Trunk Transport," MPR Archive, June 4, 1993, https://archive.mpr.org/stories/1993/06/04/update-on-police-trunk-transport. According to a June 2021 *Guardian* article, the officers did not get suspended and the city awarded Lone Eagle and Boney each $100,000. Amudalat Ajasa and Lois Beckett, "Before Chauvin: Decades of Minneapolis Police Violence That Failed to Spark Reform," *Guardian*, April 25, 2021.
10. Combs, "'City Indians' Use Art to Stake Their Claim."
11. The examples of Minnesota Indigenous artists whose work calls out or talks back to mainstream institutions is far too many to name here. One, though, is Jim Denominie (d. 2023) whose painting *Attack on Fort Snelling Bar and Grill* includes a Minneapolis Police car with a Native American man and a horse in the trunk.
12. "About This Site."
13. "'Bdote Memory Map' Provides a New Understanding of Mnisota (Minnesota) through the Eyes of Its First Residents," *Red Lake News*, October 3, 2012, https://www.redlakenationnews.com/story/2012/10/03/news/bdote-memory-map-provides-a-new-understanding-of-mnisota-minnesota-through-the-eyes-of-its-first-residents/5336.html.
14. "About This Site."
15. The story of Fort Snelling begins with Pike's Treaty, which was the "sale" of Pike Island and the surrounding area, including the site nearby where Fort Snelling was built. "Relations: Dakota and Ojibwe: Treaty with the Sioux, 1805: Signed September 23, 1805 at 'Pike Island,' Minnesota," Treaties Matter, https://treatiesmatter.org/treaties/land/1805-dakota. According to the Minnesota Historical Society:

    > Following the war of 1812, the U.S. government sought to strengthen its control over the Northwestern territories by establishing a series of forts at strategic points in the region. One of these sites was the junction of the Minnesota or St. Peter's River and the Mississippi River. In 1819, U.S. troops began building the post on the high bluff above the area where the rivers meet. The new post was named Fort Snelling for Col. Josiah Snelling, the officer who oversaw most of its construction. Besides being the crossroads of two important river "highways,"

the region around the fort had cultural and economic importance for the Dakota and Ojibwe people, thus Fort Snelling formed the economic and cultural hub of early Minnesota.

"Fort Snelling Overview," Minnesota Historical Society, https://libguides.mnhs.org/fortsnelling. Construction of the fort was completed in 1825, at which time it was renamed Fort Snelling in recognition of Colonel Snelling who had overseen construction. "Historic Fort Snelling: Learn, Timeline," Minnesota Historical Society, https://www.mnhs.org/fortsnelling/learn/timeline.

16. "MNHS: Historic Adventures," Minnesota Historical Society, https://www.mnhs.org/locations. There are recent examples of collaboration between MNHS and local Indigenous communities. Since 2007, the Lower Sioux Cansayai tribe has comanaged the Lower Sioux visitor's center. "Lower Sioux Agency Historic Site Information," Lower Sioux Community, https://lowersioux.com/departments/historic-site/. The return of 120 acres, which includes the Lower Sioux Agency historic site in March 2021, was the culmination of years of discussion between the Cansiyapi tribe, the greater Dakota community, MNHS, and the state of Minnesota. See: Minn. Law 2017, Ch. 54 § 23; Stuart Huntington, "Historic Dakota Land Returns to Tribe: Minnesota Repatriated 120 Acres to the Lower Sioux Indian Community but More Land Is Still Held by the State," *Indian Country Today*, March 29, 2021, https://ictnews.org/news/historic-dakota-land-returns-to-tribe; "Lower Sioux Agency," Minnesota Historical Society, https://www.mnhs.org/lowersioux.
17. The effects of sharing Indigenous place knowledge or sites of significance have often led to desecration of these sites. While the creation of the 1993 Native American Grave Repatriation Act has done much to stop grave robbing, incidents of desecration continue. Elizabeth Evitts Dickinson, "The Endless Robbing of Native American Graves," *Washington Post Online*, July 8, 2021, https://www.washingtonpost.com/magazine/2021/07/08/will-mass-robbery-native-american-graves-ever-end/; "Federal Agents Bust Ring of Antiquity Thieves Looting American Indian Sites for Priceless Treasures," U.S. Department of the Interior, news release, June 10, 2009, https://www.doi.gov/news/pressreleases/2009_06_10_releaseA.
18. Decommissioned in 1946 and abandoned for decades, the site deteriorated until efforts by the Minnesota Centennial Commission to preserve the remaining four of the original fifteen structures and unearth the original fort walls. The 1958 state centennial spurred military nostalgia and attention turned to Fort Snelling. The addition of the site to the National Registry in 1960 began decades of interest and monies dedicated to rebuilding the fort to appear as it did in the 1820s. This effort also resulted in altering plans for the expansion of Highway 55, which had been designed to run through the middle of

the site, to run under the site instead. Advocates for the site enjoyed consistent state attention and resources into the present day.

19. Gwen Westerman and Bruce White, *Mni Sota Makoce: The Land of the Dakota* (Saint Paul: Minnesota Historical Society Press, 2012), 20.
20. "Timeline," Minnesota Historical Society, https://www.mnhs.org/fortsnelling/learn/timeline.
21. Jessica Mader, "From Cannon Falls to St. Paul, Wagon Train Marks Sesquicentennial," Minnesota Public Radio, May 12, 2008.
22. "Protestors Meet Wagon Train," MPR News, May 10, 2008, https://www.mprnews.org/story/2008/05/10/wagonsat.
23. Jennifer Brooks, "State Senators Try to Slash Minnesota Historical Society's Budget over Sign at Fort Snelling," *Star Tribune* (Minneapolis), April 25, 2019, https://www.startribune.com/article/509070182/.
24. From the April 23, 2019, Minnesota Senate Finance Committee Meeting, Senator Kiffmeyer:

    > And, uh, it did generate a good deal of discussion amongst the members of the capital investment committee. And I was one of them following that discussion. I had a constituent of mine from my Senate district contact me and provided me with a number of, um, uh, concerns that she had regarding what the historical society was planning to do with historic Fort Snelling in terms of, uh, the exhibits in the interpretative center and so forth that they're gonna plan out there.
    >
    > And so the controversy, uh, senators, uh, revolves around whether or not the historical society is engaged in revisionist history. And that is of course, something that I very strongly oppose as a result of that, uh, uh, committee hearing.

    "Senate Webcast," Minnesota Senate, April 23, 2019, https://mnsenate.granicus.com/player/clip/4022?view_id=1&redirect=true.
25. "Reintroducing Historic Fort Snelling," Minnesota Historical Society, https://www.mnhs.org/fortsnelling/revitalization.
26. Vine Deloria Jr., *God Is Red: A Native View of Religion* (Golden: Fulcrum, 2003),66.
27. Greg Dickinson, "Space, Place, and the Textures of Rhetorical Criticism," *Western Journal of Communication* 84, no. 3 (2019): 305.
28. This commemorative ride is the one begun by Jim Miller and featured in the documentary *Dakota 38*. According to the *Mankato Free Press*, Lengkeek led the

ride from 2005 to 2009. Dan Nienaber, "Reconciliation riders, runners reach Kato," *Mankato Free Press*, December 26, 2009, https://www.mankatofreepress.com/news/local_news/reconciliation-riders-runners-reach-kato/article_c5256766-a9e6-55e3-8e1b-b827652eef6d.html. According to the *Pipestone Star*, Miller started the ride and passed on the leadership role to Lengkeek in 2008. "Dakota 38 Rides through Pipestone along 330-Mile Journey," *Pipestone Star*, December 22, 2011, https://www.pipestonestar.com/articles/dakota-38-rides-through-pipestone-along-330-mile-journey/.

29. Over six thousand linguists graduated from the Military Intelligence Service Language School (MISLS), which was originally located about twenty miles away in Camp Savage in Savage, Minnesota, and relocated to Fort Snelling. This school was established upon approval from the governor of Minnesota and shortly after the Japanese Interment Act, Executive order 9066 was issued. From "Military Intelligence Service Language School at Fort Snelling: Overview," Gale Family Library, Minnesota Historical Society.
30. Hannah Yang, "Descendants of Executed Dakota 38+2 Ride to Mankato to Honor Ancestors," *MPR News*, December 23, 2022, https://www.mprnews.org/story/2022/12/23/descendants-of-executed-dakota-382-ride-to-mankato-to-honor-ancestors.
31. It is important to note that since before the United States existed, Native Americans have served in the military. Native Americans serve at a higher proportion than any other ethnicity. According to a 2021 USO article, since 2011, 19 percent of American Indians have served in the U.S. military, compared to an average of 14 percent of other races. Danielle DeSimone, "A History of Military Service: Native Americans in the U.S. Military Yesterday and Today," United Service Organization, November 8, 2021, https://www.uso.org/stories/2914-a-history-of-military-service-native-americans-in-the-u-s-military-yesterday-and-today. According to a May 2020 U.S. Veterans Affairs report, the rate of Native Americans serving in the military was 17.7 percent compared to other ethnicities at 14 percent. Department of Veterans Affairs, *Special Report, American Indian and Alaska Native Veterans: 2017*, (Washington, D.C.: Department of Veterans Affairs, May 2020), https://www.va.gov/vetdata/docs/SpecialReports/AIAN.pdf.
32. Audra Simpson, *Mohawk Interruptus: Political Life across the Borders of Settler States* (Durham: Duke University Press, 2014), 10.
33. Mishuana Goeman, "Land as Life: Unsettling the Logics of Containment," in *Native Studies Keywords*, ed. Stephanie Nohelani Teves, Andrea Smith, and Michelle H. Raheja (Phoenix: University of Arizona Press, 2015), 74.
34. Glen S. Coulthard, "Subjects of Empire: Indigenous Peoples and the 'Politics of Recognition' in Canada," *Contemporary Political Theory* 6 (2007): 439.
35. Audra Simpson, "The Ruse of Consent and the Anatomy of 'Refusal': Cases from

Indigenous North America and Australia," *Postcolonial Studies* 20, no. 1 (2017): 19.

36. "Oheyawhi / Pilot Knob Pocket Guide," Pilot Knob Preservation Association, http://www.pilotknobpreservation.org/Pocket%20Guide%20Interactive.htm.
37. Goeman, "Land as Life," 72.
38. In the tour I took in April of 2023, the guide explained that part of the revitalization was the planting of native plants throughout the site. In the beginning of the tour, as we walked the grounds outside of the visitor's center and fort, the guide explained that "this is Dakota homeland and the prairie was a big part of their life." At the end of the nearly hour-long tour, as we stood inside of the fort, I asked the guide if there were any markers or reference to Dakota in the fort. He explained that the Dakota community had asked MNHS to allow them, the Dakota community, to tell that story. This insistence that Dakota stories of place be told by Dakota is a way of refusing recognition by MNHS and other non-Dakota institutions.
39. Fort Snelling state park was established in 1960. Samuel H. Morgan, "Birth, Death, Reincarnation: The Story of Fort Snelling and Its State Park," *Ramsey County History* 28, no. 2 (1983): 5.
40. Betasamosake Simpson, *As We Have Always Done*, 16.
41. Simpson, "The Ruse of Consent," 22.
42. This is akin to the Native Land Map, a global interactive map which shows the tribal connections to land. See: Native Land Map, https://native-land.ca/.
43. Dickinson, "Space, Place, and the Textures of Rhetorical Criticism," 302.
44. Simpson, *Mohawk Interruptus*, 22.

CONCLUSION

1. A bit of background on the relationship between the state flag and seal is useful. When Minnesota became a state in 1858, it was required to have a state seal. Governor Henry Sibley instructed Secretary of State Francis Baasen to use the former territory's seal. Sibley revised the current state seal by replacing "Quo sursum velo videre" ("I want to see what lies beyond") with "L'Etoile du Nord" ("star of the North"). According to the Minnesota Secretary of State State Seal website, Sibley also "reversed the picture on the seal to depict the sun setting in the west instead of rising in the east." Office of the Secretary of State Steve Simon, Minnesota Secretary of State, "State Seal." The exact history of the state flag is a bit trickier to trace, as an official state flag was not adopted until the 1893 World's Fair held in Chicago. Minnesota Governor William R. Merriam

tasked the "Women's Auxiliary Board" to form a subcommittee of six women who then vetted and selected a flag design. Historians examine not only the design chosen by the committee, but the flags raised by each of Minnesota's eleven infantry regiments which fought in the Civil and U.S.-Dakota War as well as the Spanish-American War. According to historian William M. Becker, multiple regiments carried a flag which bore the state seal design and "Star of the North." William M. Becker, "A Theory: The Origin of the Minnesota State Flag," *Minnesota History*, spring 1992, 2–8.

2. Becker, "A Theory: The Origin of the Minnesota State Flag," 2.
3. Kelly Smith and Briana Bierschbach, "New Minnesota State Flag Becomes Partisan Issue in 2024," *Star Tribune* (Minneapolis), January 27, 2024, https://www.startribune.com/new-state-flag-becomes-partisan-issue-in-2024/600339023/; Bill Walsh, "No One Wants a New Flag," Center for American Experiment, May 10, 2024, https://www.americanexperiment.org/thinking-minnesota-poll-no-one-wants-a-new-flag/; Fritz Bush, "Brown Co. Board OKs Resolution Opposing State Flag Redesign Process," *The Journal* (New Ulm), February 28, 2024, https://www.nujournal.com/news/local-news/2024/02/28/brown-co-board-oks-resolution-opposing-state-flag-redesign-process/; Charlene Corson Selby, "Brownsville to Continue Flying Current Minnesota State Flag," *Filmore County Journal* (Brownsville), January 8, 2024, https://fillmorecountyjournal.com/brownsville-to-continue-flying-current-minnesota-state-flag/; Renee Richardson, "Crow Wing Commissioners Split in Vote to Send Resolution Opposing New State Flag," *Brainerd Dispatch*, January 2, 2024, https://www.brainerddispatch.com/news/local/crow-wing-commissioners-split-in-vote-to-send-resolution-opposed-to-new-state-flag.
4. "Historic State Flag," Minnesota Secretary of State, https://www.sos.state.mn.us/about-minnesota/minnesota-in-profile/historic-state-flag/; "Historic State Seal," Minnesota Secretary of State, https://www.sos.state.mn.us/about-minnesota/minnesota-in-profile/historic-state-seal/.
5. William Convery, "Minnesota State Seal," *Minnopedia*, Minnesota Historical Society, https://www.mnopedia.org/thing/minnesota-state-seal.
6. Martin Case, *The Relentless Business of Treaties: How Indigenous Land Became U.S. Property* (Saint Paul: Minnesota Historical Society Press, 2018), 150; Mary Lethert Wingerd, *North Country: The Making of Minnesota* (Minneapolis: University of Minnesota Press, 2010), 183.
7. Brown v. Board of Education of Topeka, 347 U.S. 483 (1954).
8. Public Law 959, sect. 3416, ch. 930 (1956); See also Mato Canali Winyan, "Indian Relocation Act, Part One," *Lakota Times*, October 26, 2022, https://www.lakotatimes.com/articles/part-1-indian-relocation-act/; Max Nersterek, "Uprooted: The Plan to Erase

Indian Country," *American Public Media*, November 1, 2019, https://www.apmreports.org/episode/2019/11/01/uprooted-the-1950s-plan-to-erase-indian-country/.

9. "Whose Heritage? Public Symbols of the Confederacy," Southern Poverty Law Center, February 1, 2019, https://www.splcenter.org/20190201/whose-heritage-public-symbols-confederacy.
10. Kiara Alfonseca, "Derek Chauvin Sentenced to 21 Years on Federal Charges for Violating George Floyd's Civil Rights," *ABC News Go*, July 7, 2022, https://abcnews.go.com/US/derek-chauvin-sentenced-federal-charges-violating-george-floyds/story?id=86366456.
11. "Symbols of the Confederacy Removed since George Floyd's Death," Southern Poverty Law Center, https://www.splcenter.org/symbols-confederacy-removed-george-floyds-death.
12. Youjin Shin, Nick Kirkpatrick, Catherine D'Ignazio, and Wonyoung So, "Columbus Monuments Are Coming Down, but He's Still Honored in 6,000 Places across the U.S. Here's Where." *Washington Post*, October 26, 2021, https://www.washingtonpost.com/history/interactive/2021/christopher-columbus-monuments-america-map/; Kristi Miller, "Protesters Tear Down Christopher Columbus Statue on Minnesota Capitol Grounds, *Pioneer Press* (Saint Paul), June 11, 2020, https://www.twincities.com/2020/06/10/protesters-tear-down-christopher-columbus-statue-on-minnesota-capitol-grounds/; Gordon Severson, "The Fate of Minnesota's Toppled Christopher Columbus Statue Still Undecided More Than a Year Later," *Star Tribune* (Minneapolis), October 11, 2021, https://www.kare11.com/article/news/local/breaking-the-news/fate-of-minnesotas-toppled-christopher-columbus-statue-still-undecided/89-18f6701-7a99-40b7-bc45-fa7c6aa671d3; Peter Callaghan, "Mancini's Quest to Honor Italian Americans 4 Years after Toppling of State Capitol Columbus Statue," *Minnpost*, March 25, 2024, https://www.minnpost.com/state-government/2024/03/mancinis-italian-americans-minnesota-state-capitol-christopher-columbus/.
13. "How Statues Are Falling around the World," *New York Times*, June 24, 2020; "Confederate and Columbus Statues Toppled by US Protestors," *BBC News*, June 11, 2020.
14. Alan Taylor, "The Statues Brought down since the George Floyd Protests Began," *Atlantic*, July 2020.
15. "Minnesota Protesters Pull Down Columbus Statue at Capitol," *MPR News*, June 10, 2020, https://www.mprnews.org/story/2020/06/10/minnesota-protesters-pull-down-columbus-statue-at-capitol.
16. Leah Donnella, "The Standing Rock Resistance Is Unprecedented (It's Also Centuries Old)," *Code Switch*, National Public Radio, November 22, 2016.
17. According to a 2020 report to the Minnesota Legislature by the Missing and Murdered

Indigenous Women Task Force, in a 2019 American Survey report, Indigenous women and girls make up 1 percent of the state population, yet they account for 15 percent of the missing person cases in any given month in Minnesota. Nicole Martin Rogers and Virgina Pendelton, *A Report to the Minnesota Legislature by the Missing and Murdered Indigenous Women Task Force* (Saint Paul: Office of Public Safety, Office of Justice Programs, December 2020), https://dps.mn.gov/divisions/ojp/Documents/missing-murdered-indigenous-women-task-force-report.pdf. According to the Urban Indian Health Institute, Minnesota ranks ninth in the country for missing and murdered Indigenous women. Urban Indian Health Institute, *Missing and Murdered Indigenous Women and Girls: A Snapshot of Data from 71 Urban Cities in the United States* (Seattle: Urban Indian Health Institute), http://www.uihi.org/wp-content/uploads/2018/11/Missing-and-Murdered-Indigenous-Women-and-Girls-Report.pdf. According to a 2021 report by the Minnesota Department of Health, Indigenous children are 18.5 times more likely to be placed in out-of-home care. Minnesota Department of Health *American Indian Maternal and Child Health: The Health and Well-Being of American Indian Women, Children, and Families* (Saint Paul: Minnesota Department of Health, Child and Family Health Division, March 25, 2021), https://www.health.state.mn.us/docs/communities/titlev/amindian2021.pdf.

18. Kevin Jensvold, Tribal Chairperson, Upper Sioux Community, "House State and Local Government Panel hears Bill to Replace MN's Current Flag and Seal," statement to Minnesota House and Finance Committee on House File 274, February 21, 2023, YouTube, https://www.youtube.com/watch?v=IHP42ezfcE4.
19. Mike Cook, "Not up to Standard? Renewed Efforts to Replace Minnesota's State Seal, Flag Gain Steam," Minnesota House of Representatives, February 21, 2023, https://www.house.mn.gov/sessiondaily/Story/17699.
20. Tim Nelson, "Push to Change Minnesota State Flag Gains Traction, Faces Headwinds," *MPR News*, April 27, 2022, https://www.mprnews.org/story/2022/04/27/north-star-journey-minnesota-state-flag-debate?gclid=CjwKCAjw3ueiBhBmEiwA4BhspAfzEtPzesmZgvw6RcxmjyK-PSeMWsyHLfrTrxXCV9mz_b36jbILjxoCFrIQAvD_BwE.
21. The idea that icons, in this case, of industry are repeatedly reanimated in order to maintain privilege and secure resources is the heart of this film. Ted Kotcheff, dir., *Weekend at Bernie's*, 1989.The film summary from Rotten Tomatoes reads:

    > Fun-loving salesmen Richard (Jonathan Silverman) and Larry (Andrew McCarthy) are invited by their boss, Bernie (Terry Kiser), to stay the weekend at his posh beach house. Little do they know that Bernie is the perpetrator of

> a fraud they've uncovered and is arranging to have them killed. When the plan backfires and Bernie is killed instead, the buddies decide not to let a little death spoil their vacation. They pretend Bernie is still alive, leading to hijinks and corpse desecration galore.

"Weekend at Bernie's," Rotten Tomatoes, https://www.rottentomatoes.com/m/weekend_at_bernies.

22. Leanne Betasamosake Simpson, "Land as Pedagogy: Nishnaabeg Intelligence and Rebellious Transformation," *Decolonization: Indigeneity, Education & Society* 3, no. 3 (2014): 7.
23. J. Kēhaulani Kauanui, "'A Structure, Not an Event': Settler Colonialism and Enduring Indigeneity," *Lateral: A Journal of the Cultural Studies Association* 5, no. 1 (2016), https://csalateral.org/issue/5-1/forum-alt-humanities-settler-colonialism-enduring-indigeneity-kauanui/.
24. Mishuana Goeman, "Land as Life: Unsettling the Logics of Containment," in *Native Studies Keywords*, ed. Tephanie Mohelani Teves, Andrea Smith, and Michelle H. Raheja (Phoenix: University of Arizona Press, 2015), 74.
25. Leanne Betasamosake Simpson, *As We Have Always Done: Indigenous Freedom through Radical Resistance* (Minneapolis: University of Minnesota Press, 2020), 9.
26. Simpson, *Mohawk Interruptus*, 107.
27. Leanne Betasamosake Simpson, *Dancing on Our Turtle's Back: Stories of Nishnaabeg Re-Creation, Resurgence and a New Emergence* (Winnipeg: ARP Books, 2011), 11.
28. Betasamosake Simpson, *As We Have Always Done*, 50.
29. The establishment of earthen lodges required a change to zoning laws. See H.B. 1042 and S.F. 1087. These laws established a waiver for state building and fire codes for federally recognized Native American tribes. H.B. 1042 reads:

> The state fire marshal shall issue building-specific waivers for elements of the State Fire Code that conflict with a federally recognized tribe's religious beliefs, traditional building practices, or established teachings. Both individual members of federally recognized tribes, direct lineal descendents of federally recognized tribes, and organizations of members of federally recognized tribes may apply for these waivers.
>
> (b) Waivers may only be granted for the following types of buildings:
> (1) traditional residential buildings that will be used solely by an individual applicant's household or an organizational applicant's members;
> (2) meeting houses; and

(3) one-room educational buildings.

(c) To obtain a waiver, an applicant must apply to the state fire marshal on a form established by the state fire marshal. The application must:

(1) identify the building the waiver will apply to;

(2) identify the tribe the applicant is a member of; and

(3) declare that requirements of the State Fire Code conflict with religious beliefs, traditional building practices, or established teachings of the identified tribe, which the applicant adheres to.

(d) Any building for which a waiver is granted may not be sold or leased until:

(1) the building is brought into compliance with the version of the State Fire Code in force at the time of the sale or lease; or

(2) the prospective buyer or lessee to which the building is being sold or leased to obtains a waiver under this section for the building.

Office of Minnesota Legislature, Office of the Revisor of Statutes, HF 1042 1st Engrossment—92nd Legislature (2021—2022), February 11, 2022.

See also Emma Needham, "State Law and Land Recovery," *MN Native News*, April 7, 2021, https://minnesotanativenews.org/state-law-and-land-recovery/; "Their Goal to Live a Traditional, Dakota Lifestyle Will Take an Act of the Legislature," *West Central Tribune* (Granite Falls), February 28, 2020, https://www.wctrib.com/community/their-goal-to-live-a-traditional-dakota-lifestyle-will-take-an-act-of-the-legislature.

30. Historic Fort Snelling at Bdote is a national landmark owned and operated by the Minnesota Historical Society. The press kit highlights the fact that the recently restored Plank visitor center is over twenty thousand square feet, but does not specify the total acreage or borders of the MNHS site. Minnesota Historic Fort Snelling at Bdote, Press Kit, https://www.mnhs.org/media/kits/fortsnelling. The adjacent Fort Snelling State Park is owned by the National Park Service and operated by the Minnesota Department of Natural Resources. "Fort Snelling State Park: Mississippi National River & Recreation Area," National Park Service, https://www.nps.gov/places/fort-snelling-state-park.htm.

31. Audra Simpson, "The Ruse of Consent and the Anatomy of 'Refusal': Cases from Indigenous North America and Australia," *Postcolonial Studies* 20, no. 1 (2017): 29.

32. It is difficult to catalogue all of the changes that the Walker made following *Scaffold*. Using the search term "Native American" on the Walker website yields 946 results. Here is a sampling: "Beyond the Guest Appearance: Native Arts Panel," Walker Art Center, April 12, 2018, https://walkerart.org/magazine/panel-discussion-native-arts-nicholas-galanin-ashley-holland-candice-hopkins-steven-loft; and, more recently, "Mack Lecture:

Sterlin Harjo," Walker Art Center, June 12, 2024, https://walkerart.org/calendar/2024/mack-lecture-sterlin-harjo.

33. Simpson, *Mohawk Interruptus*, 20.
34. Glen S. Coulthard, *Red Skin, White Masks: Rejecting the Colonial Politics of Recognition* (Minneapolis: University of Minnesota Press, 2014), 27.
35. See, for recent example, "MnDOT Redesigning Highway 23 Project after Damaging Native American Burial Site," *Red Lake Nation News*, August 9, 2017, https://www.redlakenationnews.com/story/2017/08/09/news/mndot-redesigning-highway-23-project-after-damaging-native-american-burial-site/63443.html; Curt Brown, "A Dispute with a View: Pilot Knob Hill," *Star Tribune* (Minneapolis), February 28, 2003, B1; Shelby Lindrud, "Burial Ground Discovered under Kandiyohi County Park Raises Maintenance Questions," *West Central Tribune* (Granite Falls), February 28, 2024.
36. Brian Newland, *Federal Indian Boarding School Initiative Investigative Report, Vol. II* (Washington, D.C.: Bureau of Indian Affairs, July 2024), https://www.bia.gov/sites/default/files/media_document/doi_federal_indian_boarding_school_initiative_investigative_report_vii_final_508_compliant.pdf.
37. Betasamosake Simpson, *As We Have Always Done*, 16, 197.
38. See, for example, Christine Diindiisi McCleave, "Healing with Two Spirit and Native LGBTQ+ Relatives," National Native American Boarding School Healing Coalition, June 29, 2020, https://boardingschoolhealing.org/healing-with-two-spirit-and-native-lgbtq-relatives/. See, for example, Mark Rifkin, *When Did Indians Become Straight? Kinship, the History of Sexuality, and Native Sovereignty* (London: Oxford University Press, 2011).
39. Lisa King, "Competition, Complicity, and (Potential) Alliance: Native Hawaiian and Asian Immigrant Narratives at the Bishop Museum," *College Literature: A Journal of Critical Literary Studies* 41, no. 1 (2014): 57.
40. Bruce White, "Tearing Down Fort Snelling—Why It Makes Sense." *Star Tribune* (Minneapolis), April 9, 2009.
41. Kay Anderson and Mona Domosh, "North American Spaces/Postcolonial Stories," *Cultural Geographies* 9 (2002): 126.
42. Dickinson, "Space, Place, and the Textures of Rhetorical Criticism," 307.
43. Michael Lechuga, "An Anticolonial Future: Reassembling the Way We Do Rhetoric," *Communication and Critical/Cultural Studies* 17, no. 4 (2020): 380.
44. I recognize the potential scope of this indictment. I make this argument in the spirit of scholarship and its role in generating sometimes difficult but often therefore critical discussion. In short, I leave it to my community of scholars and activists to reflect on their own research and efforts guided by the question of what compels our work and the

degree to which it serves communities and that to which it builds our own intellectual and/or professional cache. If I take a hard position on this, all studies of place that have been carried out without the permission of members of the Indigenous communities who hold a relationship with said place are guilty of extractionist research. I rely on Indigenous Studies scholar Linda Tuhiwai Smith, who focuses not on method but the "context in which research problems are conceptualized and designed, and with the implications of research for its participants and their communities." Linda Tuhiwai Smith, *Decolonizing Methodologies: Research and Indigenous Peoples* (New York: Zed Books, 2012), ix. Tuhiwai Smit's point turns the question back on the individual researcher's relationship building with Indigenous communities who have a relationship with said place. Documenting evidence of whether or not that permission has been sought and granted is complicated, too, because of publication format and guidelines. The strictures of publishing do not generally allow for discussion of or attention to the role of relationships between Indigenous people and research.

45. Coulthard, *Red Skin, White Masks*, 61.
46. Tiara Na'puti, "Oceanic Possibilities for Communication Studies," *Communication and Critical/Cultural Studies* 17, no. 1 (2020): 496.
47. Lorenzo Veracini, "Decolonizing Settler Colonialism: Kill the Settler in Him and Save the Man," *American Indian Culture and Research Journal* 41, no. 1 (2017): 9.
48. Christine Elers and Mohan Dutta, "Academic-Community Solidarities in Land Occupation as an Indigenous Claim to Health: Culturally Centered Solidarity through Voice Infrastructures," *Frontiers in Communication* 8, no. (2023).

Works Cited

Aden, Roger C. "When Memories and Discourses Collide: The President's House and Places of Public Memory." *Communication Monographs* 79, no. 1 (2012): 72–92.

Ajasa, Amudalat, and Lois Beckett. "Before Chauvin: Decades of Minneapolis Police Violence that Failed to Spark Reform." *Guardian*, April 25, 2021.

Alfonseca, Kiara. "Derek Chauvin Sentenced to 21 Years on Federal Charges for Violating George Floyd's Civil Rights." *ABC News Go*, July 7, 2022. https://abcnews.go.com/US/derek-chauvin-sentenced-federal-charges-violating-george-floyds/story?id=86366456.

Alfred, Taiaiake. "What Is Radical Imagination? Indigenous Struggles in Canada." *Affinities: A Journal of Radical Theory, Culture, and Action* 4, no. 2 (Fall 2010): 5–8.

"A Mall of America Flash Mob for First Nations' Rights." *YES!*, January 5, 2013. https://www.yesmagazine.org/democracy/2013/01/05/mall-of-america-flash-mob-first-nations-rights-idle-no-more.

Anderson, Gary C. *Kinsmen of Another Kind: Dakota-White Relations in the Upper Mississippi Valley, 1650–1862*. Saint Paul: Minnesota Historical Society Press, 1997.

———. *Little Crow: Spokesman for the Sioux*. Saint Paul: Minnesota Historical Society Press, 1986.

Anderson, Kay, and Mona Domosh. "North American Spaces/Postcolonial Stories." *Cultural*

Geographies 9 (2002): 125–128.

Anderson, Ryan. "Century Farm: Krause Family Honored as Century Farm." *Faribault Daily News*, October 12, 2018.

Asante, Godfried A. "#RhetoricSoWhite and US Centered: Reflections on Challenges and Opportunities." *Quarterly Journal of Speech* 104, no. 4 (2019): 484–488.

Barker, Adam J. "Locating Settler Colonialism." *Journal of Colonialism and Colonial History* 13, no. 3 (2012), https://doi.org/10.1353/cch.2012.0035.

Beane, Katherine E. "Woyakapi Kin Ahdipi 'Bringing the Story Home': A History Within the Wakpa Ipaksan Dakota Oyate." Doctoral dissertation, University of Minnesota, 2014.

Becker, William M. "A Theory: The Origin of the Minnesota State Flag." *Minnesota History*, spring 1992, 2–8.

Betasamosake Simpson, Leanne. "Aambe! Maajaadaa! (What #Idlenomore Means to Me)." *Decolonization: Indigeneity, Education and Society*, December 21, 2012.

———. *As We Have Always Done: Indigenous Freedom through Radical Resistance.* Minneapolis: University of Minnesota Press, 2020.

———. *Dancing on Our Turtle's Back: Stories of Nishnaabeg Re-Creation, Resurgence and a New Emergence*. Winnipeg: ARP Books, 2011.

———. "Indigenous Resurgence and Co-Resistance." *Critical Ethnic Studies* 2, no. 2. (2016): 19–34.

———. "Land as Pedagogy: Nishnaabeg Intelligence and Rebellious Transformation." *Decolonization: Indigeneity, Education & Society* 3, no. 3 (2014): 1–25.

"'Bdote Memory Map' Provides a New Understanding of Mnisota (Minnesota) through the Eyes of its First Residents." *Red Lake News*, October 3, 2012. https://www.redlakenationnews.com/story/2012/10/03/news/bdote-memory-map-provides-a-new-understanding-of-mnisota-minnesota-through-the-eyes-of-its-first-residents/5336.html.

Black, Jason. "Indigenizing the Rhetoric and Public Address Classroom: Memory as a Native American Discursive Tactic." *Communication Teacher* 27, no. 1 (2013): 21–28.

Blair, Carole. "Reflections on Criticism and Bodies: Parables from Public Places." *Western Journal of Communication* 65, no. 3 (2001): 271–294, doi:10.1080/10570310109374706.

Blair, Carole, Greg Dickinson, and Brian Ott. "Introduction: Rhetoric/Memory/Place." In *Places of Public Memory: The Rhetoric of Museums and Memorials*, edited by Greg Dickinson, Carole Blair, and Brian Ott, 1–54. Tuscaloosa: University of Alabama Press, 2010.

Blair, Carole, Marsha S. Jeppeson, and Enrico Pucci Jr. "Public Memorializing in Postmodernity: The Vietnam Veterans Memorial as Prototype." *Quarterly Journal of Speech* 77 (1991): 263–288.

Booth, William J. "Economies of Time: On the Idea of Time in Marx's Political Economy."

Political Theory 19, no. 1 (1991): 7–27.

Bowman, Emma, Bill Chapell, and Becky Sullivan. "What We Know So Far about the Buffalo Mass Shootings." National Public Radio, May 22, 2022. https://www.npr.org/2022/05/15/1099028397/buffalo-shooting-what-we-know.

Brooks, Jennifer. "State Senators Try to Slash Minnesota Historical Society's Budget over Sign at Fort Snelling." *Star Tribune* (Minneapolis), April 25, 2019.

Brown, Curt. "A Dispute with a View: Pilot Knob Hill." *Star Tribune* (Minneapolis), February 28, 2003, B1.

———. "Little Crow's Legacy." *Star Tribune* (Minneapolis), August 17, 2012.

Brown, Nicholas, and Sarah E. Kanouse. *Re-Collecting Black Hawk: Landscape, Memory, and Power in the American Midwest.* Pittsburgh: University of Pittsburgh Press, 2015.

Browing, Dan. "Minnesota's 'Century Farms' Total Nearly 11,000." *Star Tribune* (Minneapolis), April 13, 2019.

Bruce, Caitlin F. "River of Words as Space for Encounter: Contested Meaning in Rhetorical Convergence Zones." *Quarterly Journal of Speech* 105, no. 4 (2019): 441–464.

Bruyneel, Kevin. "Wake Work versus Work of Settler Memory: Modes of Solidarity in #NoDAPL, Black Lives Matter, and Anti-Trumpism." In *Standing with Standing Rock: Voices from the #NoDAPL Movement*, edited by Nick Estes and Jaskiran Dhillon, 311–327. Minneapolis: University of Minnesota Press, 2019.

Bush, Fritz. "Brown Co. Board OKs Resolution Opposing State Flag Redesign Process." *The Journal* (New Ulm), February 28, 2024.

Byrd, Jodi. *The Transit of Empire: Indigenous Critiques of Colonialism.* Minneapolis: University of Minnesota Press, 2011.

Callaghan, Peter. "Mancini's Quest to Honor Italian Americans 4 Years after Toppling of State Capitol Columbus Statue." *Minnpost*, March 25, 2024. https://www.minnpost.com/state-government/2024/03/mancinis-italian-americans-minnesota-state-capitol-christopher-columbus/.

Canali Winyan, Mato. "Li'la Wota'ku'ye Ota'pi." *Lakota Times*, February 8, 2023. https://www.lakotatimes.com/articles/lila-wotakuye-otapi/.

———. "Part One: The Indian Relocation Act." *Lakota Times*, October 26, 2022. https://www.lakotatimes.com/articles/part-1-indian-relocation-act/.

Carley, Kenneth. *The Dakota War of 1862: Minnesota's Other Civil War.* Saint Paul: Minnesota Historical Society Press, 2001.

———. *The Sioux Uprising of 1862.* Saint Paul: Minnesota Historical Society Press, 1976.

Carlson, Kelsey M. "'We'd Always Return to This Center': Understanding Urban Space as a Dakota Place in Mni Sota Makoce." Master's thesis, Syracuse University, 2015.

Carpenter, Ronald H. "Frederick Jackson Turner and the Rhetorical Impact of the Frontier Thesis." *Quarterly Journal of Speech* 63 (1977): 117–129.

Case, Martin. *The Relentless Business of Treaties: How Indigenous Land Became U.S. Property.* Saint Paul: Minnesota Historical Society Press, 2018.

Chalmers, Jason. "Settled Memories on Stolen Land: Settler Mythology at Canada's National Holocaust Museum." *American Indian Quarterly* 43 no. 4 (Fall 2019): 379–407.

Champagne, Duane. "American Indian Studies Is for Everyone." *American Indian Quarterly* 20, no. 1 (1996): 77–82, https://www.jstor.org/stable/1184943.

Chavez, Aliyah. "History Restored: Family Celebrates Return of Bde Maka Ska Lake Name." *Indian Country Today*, May 14, 2020. https://indiancountrytoday.com/news/history-restored-family-celebrates-return-of-bde-maka-ska-lake-name-zIUe198vhk6KnW1icY8SYw.

Child, Brenda J. *Holding Our World Together: Ojibwe Women and the Survival of Community.* New York: Penguin Books, 2012.

Chomsky, Carol. "The United States-Dakota War Trials: A Study in Military Injustice." *Stanford Law Review* 43, no. 13 (1990): 13–98.

Clark, D., Anthony Tyeeme, and Malea Powell. "Resisting Exile in the 'Land of the Free': Indigenous Groundwork at Colonial Intersections." *American Indian Quarterly* 32, no. 1 (2008): 1–15.

Coleman, Nick, and John Camp. "The Great Dakota Conflict." *St. Paul Pioneer Press Dispatch*, April 26, 1988.

Combs, Mariane. "'City Indians' Uses Art to Stake Their Claim." *MPR News*, November 15, 2006. https://www.mprnews.org/story/2006/11/15/cityindians.

"Concept Master Plan: Historic Murphy's Landing." Shakopee City Council, general meeting, general business. January 25, 2007. https://forms.shakopeemn.gov/WebLink/DocView.aspx?id=101968&dbid=0&repo=Shakopee.

"Confederate and Columbus Statues Toppled by US Protestors." *BBC News*, June 11, 2020. https://www.bbc.co.uk/news/world-us-canada-53005243.

Cook, Mike. "Not up to Standard? Renewed Efforts to Replace Minnesota's State Seal, Flag Gain Steam." Minnesota House of Representatives, February 21, 2023. https://www.house.mn.gov/sessiondaily/Story/17699.

Coulthard, Glen. "From Wards of the State to Subjects of Recognition? Marx, Indigenous Peoples, and the Politics of Dispossession in Denendeh." In *Theorizing Native Studies*, ed. Audra Simpson and Andrea Smith, 56–98. Durham: Duke University Press, 2014.

———. *Red Skin, White Masks: Rejecting the Colonial Politics of Recognition.* Minneapolis: University of Minnesota Press, 2014.

———. "Subjects of Empire: Indigenous Peoples and the 'Politics of Recognition' in Canada." *Contemporary Political Theory* 6 (2007): 456.

Coulthard, Glen, and Leanne Betasamosake Simpson. "Grounded Normativity and Place-Based Solidarity." *American Quarterly* 68, no. 2 (2016): 249–255.

Crosby, Andrew, and Jeffrey Monaghan. "Settler Colonialism and the Policing of Idle No More." *Social Justice* 43, no. 2 (2016): 37–57.

Crow, Reyna. "Mall of America Threatens Arrest of Idle No More Organizers if New Years Eve Round Dance Occurs—Idle No More." *Idle No More*, December 25, 2013. https://idlenomore.ca/mall-of-america-threatens-arrest-of-idle-no-more-organizers-if-new-years-eve-round-dance-occurs-idle-no-more/.

Crow, Reyna, and Sarah LittleRedfeather. "Idle No More New Year's Eve Round Dance at Mall of America." *Last Real Indians*, December 31, 2013. https://lastrealindians.com/news/2013/12/31/dec-31-2013-for-immediate-release-idle-no-more-new-years-eve-round-dance-at-mall-of-america.

"Dakota Commemorative March Retraces 150 Miles of Forced March." *The Circle*, December 16, 2012. https://thecirclenews.org/urban-news/dakota-commemorative-march-retraces-150-miles-of-forced-march/.

"Dakota 38 Rides through Pipestone along 330-mile Journey." *Pipestone Star*, December 22, 2011.

Deloria, Philip J. *Playing Indian*. New Haven: Yale University Press, 1998.

Deloria, Vine, Jr. *For This Land: Writings on Religion in America*. New York: Routledge, 1999.

———. *God Is Red: A Native View of Religion*. Golden: Fulcrum, 2003.

———. *The Metaphysics of Modern Existence*. Colorado Springs: Fulcrum, 2012.

———. *Spirit and Reason: The Vine Deloria Jr. Reader*. Golden: Fulcrum, 1999.

Deloria, Vine, Jr., and Daniel Wildcat. *Power and Place: Indian Education in America*. Golden: Fulcrum, 2001.

Department of Veterans Affairs. *Special Report, American Indian and Alaska Native Veterans: 2017*. Washington, D.C.: Department of Veterans Affairs, May 2020. https://www.va.gov/vetdata/docs/SpecialReports/AIAN.pdf.

DeSimone, Danielle. "A History of Military Service: Native Americans in the U.S. Military Yesterday and Today." United Service Organization, November 8, 2021. https://www.uso.org/stories/2914-a-history-of-military-service-native-americans-in-the-u-s-military-yesterday-and-today.

Dickinson, Elizabeth Evitts. "The Endless Robbing of Native American Graves." *Washington Post Online*, July 8, 2021. https://www.washingtonpost.com/magazine/2021/07/08/will-mass-robbery-native-american-graves-ever-end/.

Dickinson, Greg. "Memories for Sale: Nostalgia and the Construction of Identity in Old Pasadena." *Quarterly Journal of Speech* 88 (1997): 1–27.

———. "Space, Place, and the Textures of Rhetorical Criticism." *Western Journal of Communication* 84, no. 3 (2019): 297–313.

Dickinson, Greg, Brian L. Ott, and Eric Aoki. "Memory and Myth at the Buffalo Bill Museum." *Western Journal of Communication* 69, no. 2 (2005): 85–108.

Diindiisi McCleave, Christine. "Healing with Two Spirit and Native LGBTQ+ Relatives." National Native American Boarding School Healing Coalition, June 29, 2020. https://boardingschoolhealing.org/healing-with-two-spirit-and-native-lgbtq-relatives/.

Donnella, Leah. "The Standing Rock Resistance Is Unprecedented (It's Also Centuries Old)." *Code Switch*, National Public Radio, November 22, 2016.

Durant, Sam. "A Statement from Sam Durant." *Walker Magazine*, May 29, 2017. https://walkerart.org/magazine/a-statement-from-sam-durant-05-29-17.

Ek, Casey. "Dakota 38 Memorial Run Still Going Strong." *Henderson Independent*, January 1, 2020.

Eler, Alicia. "2017 Moments: 'Scaffold' Ignited a Debate about Art and Cultural Appropriation." *Star Tribune* (Minneapolis), December 28, 2017.

Elers, Christine, and Mohan Dutta. "Academic-Community Solidarities in Land Occupation as an Indigenous Claim to Health: Culturally Centered Solidarity through Voice Infrastructures." *Frontiers in Communication* 8, no. (2023). https://www.frontiersin.org/journals/communication/articles/10.3389/fcomm.2023.1009837/full.

Enck-Wanzer [Wanzer-Serrano], Darell. "Decolonizing Imaginaries: Rethinking 'the People' in the Young Lords' Church Offensive." *Quarterly Journal of Speech* 98, no. 1 (2012): 1–23. https://doi.org/10.1080/00335630.2011.638656.

Endres, Danielle. "American Indian Permission for Mascots: Resistance or Complicity within Rhetorical Colonialism?" *Rhetoric & Public Affairs* 18, no. 4: 649–690.

Endres, Danielle, and Samantha Senda-Cook. "Location Matters: The Rhetoric of Place in Protest." *Quarterly Journal of Speech* 97, no. 3 (2011): 257–282.

Estes, Nick. *Our History Is the Future: Standing Rock versus the Dakota Access Pipeline, and the Long Tradition of Indigenous Resistance*. New York: Verso, 2019.

Fabian, Johannes. *Time and the Other: How Anthropology Makes Its Object*. New York: Columbia University Press, 2002.

Fairbanks, Ashley. "Genocide and Mini-Golf in the Walker Sculpture Garden." *City Pages*, May 27, 2017.

"Farm Bureau Recognizes Sesquicentennial Farms." *Winona Post* (MN), April 15, 2020.

"Federal Agents Bust Ring of Antiquity Thieves Looting American Indian Sites for Priceless

Treasures." U.S. Department of the Interior. News release, June 10, 2009. https://www.doi.gov/news/pressreleases/2009_06_10_releaseA.

Flores, Lisa. "Advancing a Decolonial Rhetoric." *Advances in the History of Rhetoric* 21, no. 3 (2018): 320–322, https://doi.org/10.1080/15362426.2018.1526550.

Gallagher, Victoria J. "Memory and Reconciliation in the Birmingham Civil Rights Institute." *Rhetoric & Public Affairs* 2, no. 2 (1999): 303–320.

García, Romeo, and Damían Baca, eds. *Rhetorics of Elsewhere and Otherwise: Contested Modernities, Decolonial Visions*. Urbana, IL: Conference on College Composition and Communication of the National Teachers of English, 2019.

Goeman, Mishuana. "Land as Life: Unsettling the Logics of Containment." In *Native Studies Keywords*, edited by Stephanie Nohelani Teves, Andrea Smith, and Michelle H. Raheja, 71–89. Phoenix: University of Arizona Press, 2015.

Goodyear-Ka'ōpua, Noelani. *The Seeds We Planted: Portraits of a Native Hawaiian Charter School*. Minneapolis: University of Minnesota Press, 2020.

Gottdiener, M. "A Marx for Our Time: Henri Lefebvre and the Production of Space." *Sociological Theory* 11, no. 1 (1983): 129–134.

Gould, Stephen Jay. *Time's Arrow, Time's Cycle: Myth and Metaphor in the Discovery of Geological Time*. Cambridge, MA: Harvard University Press, 1987.

Gunderson, Dan, Elizabeth Dunbar, and Jiwon Choi. "A Look at Minnesota Farming in Seven Charts." *MPR News*, April 11, 2019.

Harlow, Tim. "History Will Live on at Murphy's Landing: Three Rivers Park District Has Taken Over the Shakopee Attraction." *Star Tribune* (Minneapolis), May 8, 2002.

———. "Rising from the Ashes: In the Wake of an Off-Season Fire, Volunteers Will Keep Living History Going at Murphy's Landing." *Star Tribune* (Minneapolis), May 25, 2001.

Harvey, Matthew. March 2020. "Fatal Encounters Between Native Americans and the Police." The Center for Indian Country Development, Minneapolis Federal Reserve. https://www.minneapolisfed.org/article/2020/fatal-encounters-between-native-americans-and-the-police.

Hayden, Michael Edison, Hannah Gais, Cassie Miller, Megan Squire, and Jason Wilson. "Unite the Right Five Years Later: Where Are They Now?" Southern Poverty Law Center, August 11, 2022. https://www.splcenter.org/hatewatch/2022/08/11/unite-right-5-years-later-where-are-they-now.

Hillard, Gloria. "Urban American Indians Rewrite Relocation's Legacy." National Public Radio, January 7, 2012. https://www.npr.org/2012/01/07/143800287/urban-american-indians-rewrite-relocations-legacy.

"How Statues Are Falling around the World." *New York Times*, June 24, 2020.

Hoxie, Frederick. "Retrieving the Red Continent: Settler Colonialism and the History of American Indians in the US." *Ethnic and Racial Studies* 31, no. 6 (2008): 1153–1167.

———. *Talking Back to Civilization: Indian Voices from the Progressive Era*. New York: Bedford, 2001.

Huntington, Stuart. "Historic Dakota Land Returns to Tribe: Minnesota Repatriated 120 Acres to the Lower Sioux Indian Community but More Land Is Still Held by the State." *Indian Country Today*, March 29, 2021. https://ictnews.org/news/historic-dakota-land-returns-to-tribe.

"Investigation into the City of Minneapolis and the Minneapolis Police Department." Minnesota Department of Human Rights. April 27, 2022. https://mn.gov/mdhr/assets/Investigation%20into%20the%20City%20of%20Minneapolis%20and%20the%20Minneapolis%20Police%20Department_tcm1061-526417.pdf.

Jefferson, Thomas. "Notes on Virginia." In *The Life and Selected Writings of Thomas Jefferson*, edited by Adriene Koch and William Peden, 187–288. New York: Modern Library, 1944.

Katriel, Tamar. "Sites of Memory: Discourses of the Past in Israeli Pioneering Settlement Museums." *Quarterly Journal of Speech* 80, no. 1 (1994): 1–20.

Kauanui, J. Kēhaulani. "'A Structure, Not an Event': Settler Colonialism and Enduring Indigeneity." *Lateral: A Journal of the Cultural Studies Association* 5, no. 1 (2016). https://csalateral.org/issue/5-1/forum-alt-humanities-settler-colonialism-enduring-indigeneity-kauanui/.

Kelly, Casey Ryan, and Jason Edward Black, eds. *Decolonizing Native American Rhetoric: Communicating Self-Determination*. New York: Peter Lang, 2018.

King, Lisa. "Competition, Complicity, and (Potential) Alliance: Native Hawaiian and Asian Immigrant Narratives at the Bishop Museum." *College Literature: A Journal of Critical Literary Studies* 41, no. 1 (2014): 43–65.

Klein, Naomi. "Dancing the World into Being: A Conversation with Idle No More's Leanne Simpson." *Yes! Magazine*, March 6, 2013. https://www.yesmagazine.org/social-justice/2013/03/06/dancing-the-world-into-being-a-conversation-with-idle-no-more-leanne-simpson.

Kopas, Anne. "Jacobson Farm a Marker of Dairy Life in Decades Gone By." *Faribault Daily News*, October 3, 2019.

Kotajarvi, Lauren. "Sesquicentennial Farm Carries on for Six Generations." *Post-Bulletin*, June 20, 2016.

Kotcheff, Ted, dir. *Weekend at Bernie's*. 1989.

Kuftinec, Sonja. "[Walking Through a] Ghost Town: Cultural Hauntologie in Mostar, Bosnia-Herzegovina or Mostar: A Performance Review." *Text and Performance Quarterly* 18

(1998): 81–95.

Lawhon, Judy. “Celebrating One Farm, One Family, 100 Years.” *White Bear Lake Press* (MN), July 23, 2008.

Lechuga, Michael. “An Anticolonial Future: Reassembling the Way We Do Rhetoric.” *Communication and Critical/Cultural Studies* 17, no. 4 (2020): 378–385.

———. *Visions of Invasion: Alien Affects, Cinema, and Citizenship in Settler Colonies.* Jackson: University of Mississippi Press, 2023.

Lefebvre, Henri. *The Production of Space.* Translated by Donald Nicholson-Smith. Malden, MA: Blackwell, 1984.

LeMay, Konnie. “Dakota Elders Will Oversee Dismantling, Burning of ‘Scaffold.’” *Indian Country Today*, June 1, 2017. https://newsmaven.io/indiancountrytoday/archive/dakota-elders-will-oversee-dismantling-burning-of-scaffold-19_sDGCaf0O1hDGe0q80Wg.

———. “*Scaffold* Sculpture Taints Memory of Dakota 38, Prompts Protests.” *Indian Country Today*, May 30, 2017. https://ictnews.org/archive/scaffold-sculpture-taints-memory-dakota-38-prompts-protests.

Lindrud, Shelby. “Burial Ground Discovered under Kandiyohi County Park Raises Maintenance Questions.” *West Central Tribune* (Granite Falls), February 28, 2024.

Locke, John. *Second Treatise on Property*. New York: Blackwell, 1948.

Logan, Tricia E. “Memory, Erasure, and National Myth.” In *Colonial Genocide in Indigenous North America*, edited by Andres Woolford, Jeff Benvenuto, and Alexander Laban Hinton, 149–165. Durham: Duke University Press, 2014.

Mader, Jessica. “From Cannon Falls to St. Paul, Wagon Train Marks Sesquicentennial.” Minnesota Public Radio, May 12, 2008.

Maldonado, Chandra Ann. “Commemorative (Dis)Placement: On the Limits of Textual Adaptability and the Future of Public Memory Scholarship.” *Rhetoric & Public Affairs* 24, no. 1–2 (2021): 239–252.

Maple, Emily, E. Gerald, and Lisa O’Brien. “Focus on the Collection—Decoding Jim Denomie’s Attack on Fort Snelling Bar and Grill.” *Wiesman Art Museum News*, September 1, 2012. https://wam.umn.edu/2012/09/01/focus-on-the-collection-decoding-jim-denomies-attack-on-fort-snelling-bar-and-grill/.

Martin Rogers, Nicole, and Virgina Pendelton. *A Report to the Minnesota Legislature by the Missing and Murdered Indigenous Women Task Force*. Saint Paul: Office of Public Safety, Office of Justice Programs, December 2020. https://s3.us-east-2.amazonaws.com/assets.dps.mn.gov/s3fs-public/migrated-files/divisions/ojp/Documents/missing-murdered-indigenous-women-task-force-report.pdf.

Marx, Karl. *Capital*. Vol. 1. New York: Vintage, 1973.

Mazon, David. "'Second in Line to Bury White Supremacy': Take 'Em Down Nola, Monument Removal, and Residual Memory." *Quarterly Journal of Speech* 106, no. 1 (2020): 48–71.

McCue-Enser, Margret. "Ada Deer and the Menominee Restoration: Rethinking Native American Protest Rhetoric." *Argumentation* 53, no. 1 (2017): 59–76.

McGeough, Ryan Erik, Catherine Helen Palczewski, and Randall A. Lake. "Oppositional Memory Practices as Arguments over Public Memory." *Argumentation and Advocacy* 51 (Spring 2015): 231–254.

Middleton, Michael, Aaron Hess, Danielle Endres, and Samantha Senda-Cook. *Participatory Critical Rhetoric: Theoretical and Methodological Foundations for Studying Rhetoric in Situ.* Lanham: Lexington Books, 2015.

Middleton, Michael K., Samantha Senda-Cook, and Danielle Endres. "Articulating Rhetorical Field Methods: Challenges and Tensions." *Western Journal of Communication* 75, no. 4 (2011): 386–406, doi:10.1080/10570314.2011.586969.

Mihesuah, Devon A. *So You Want to Write about American Indians? A Guide for Writers, Students, and Scholars.* Lincoln: University of Nebraska Press, 2005.

Miller, Kristi. "Protesters Tear Down Christopher Columbus Statue on Minnesota Capitol Grounds." *Pioneer Press* (Saint Paul), June 11, 2020. https://www.twincities.com/2020/06/10/protesters-tear-down-christopher-columbus-statue-on-minnesota-capitol-grounds/.

Minelli, Patrick. "Council Seeks Options on Issues of Management at Murphy's Landing." *Shakopee Valley News*, July 29, 1987: 1.

"Minneapolis Renames Intersection to Honor George Floyd." *CBS News*, May 26, 2022. https://www.cbsnews.com/news/minneapolis-renames-intersection-to-honor-george-floyd/.

Minnesota Department of Health. *American Indian Maternal and Child Health: The Health and Well-Being of American Indian Women, Children, and Families.* (Saint Paul: Minnesota Department of Health, Child and Family Health Division, March 25, 2021). https://www.health.state.mn.us/docs/communities/titlev/amindian2021.pdf.

Minnesota Historical Society. "Military Intelligence Service Language School at Fort Snelling: Overview." Gale Family Library, Minnesota Historical Society.

"Minnesota Protesters Pull Down Columbus Statue at Capitol." *MPR News*, June 10, 2020. https://www.mprnews.org/story/2020/06/10/minnesota-protesters-pull-down-columbus-statue-at-capitol.

"MnDOT Redesigning Highway 23 Project after Damaging Native American Burial Site." *Red Lake Nation News*, August 9, 2017. https://www.redlakenationnews.com/story/2017/08/09/news/mndot-redesigning-highway-23-project-after-damaging-native-american-burial-site/63443.html.

Monkman, Lenard. "Jingle Dress Dancers Honour George Floyd at Site Where He Was Killed." Canadian Broadcasting Corporation, June 2, 2020. https://www.cbc.ca/news/indigenous/jingle-dress-dancers-george-floyd-1.5595483.

Moreton-Robinson, Aileen. *Critical Indigenous Studies: Engagements in First World Locations*. Tucson: University of Arizona Press, 2016.

Morgan, Samuel H. "Birth, Death, Reincarnation: The Story of Fort Snelling and Its State Park." *Ramsey County History* 28, no. 2 (1983): 4–12.

Na'puti, Tiara R. "Oceanic Possibilities for Communication Studies." *Communication and Critical/Cultural Studies* 17, no. 1 (2020): 95–103.

———. "Speaking of Indigeneity: Navigating Genealogies against Erasure and #RhetoricSoWhite." *Quarterly Journal of Speech* 105, no. 4 (2010): 495–501.

Na'puti, Tiara R., and Judy Rohrer. "Pacific Moves beyond Colonialism: A Conversation from Hawai'i and Guåhan." *Feminist Studies* 43, no. 3 (2017): 537–547.

Needham, Emma. "State Law and Land Recovery." *MN Native News*, April 7, 2021. https://minnesotanativenews.org/state-law-and-land-recovery/.

Nelson, Tim. "Push to Change Minnesota State Flag Gains Traction, Faces Headwinds." *MPR News*, April 27, 2022. https://www.mprnews.org/story/2022/04/27/north-star-journey-minnesota-state-flag-debate?gclid=CjwKCAjw3ueiBhBmEiwA4BhspAfzEtPzesmZgvw6RcxmjyK-PSeMWsyHLfrTrxXCV9mz_b36jbILjxoCFrIQAvD_BwE.

Ness, Immanuel. *Encyclopedia of American Social Movements*. New York: Routledge, 2004.

Nesterack, Max. "Uprooted: The 1950s Plan to Erase Indian Country." *MPR News*, November 4, 2019. https://www.mprnews.org/story/2019/11/04/uprooted-the-1950s-plan-to-erase-indian-country.

Newland, Brian. *Federal Indian Boarding School Initiative Investigative Report, Vol. II*. Washington, D.C.: Bureau of Indian Affairs, July 2024. https://www.bia.gov/sites/default/files/media_document/doi_federal_indian_boarding_school_initiative_investigative_report_vii_final_508_compliant.pdf.

Nichols, Robert. *Theft Is Property: Dispossession & Critical Theory*. Durham: Duke University Press, 2020.

Nienaber, Dan. "Reconciliation Riders, Runners Reach Kato." *Mankato Free Press*, December 26, 2009. https://www.mankatofreepress.com/news/local_news/reconciliation-riders-runners-reach-kato/article_c5256766-a9e6-55e3-8e1b-b827652eef6d.html.

O'Connell, Tom. "Minnesota Farmer-Labor Party, 1924–1944." *MNOpedia*, January 5, 2024. https://www.mnopedia.org/minnesota-farmer-labor-party-1924-1944.

Oehler, Chester M. *The Great Sioux Uprising*. New York: Oxford University, 1997.

Ono, Kent A. "Darrel Wanzer-Serrano's the New Young Lords and the Struggle for Liberation:

Theoretical Contributions." *Advances in the History of Rhetoric* 21, no. 3 (2018): 315–319, https://doi.org/10.1080/15362426.2018.1526549.

Ortiz, Roxanne Dunbar, ed. *The Great Sioux Nation: Sitting in Judgement on America; An Oral History of the Sioux Nation and Its Struggle for Sovereignty.* Lincoln: Bison Books, 2013.

Paliewicz, Nicholas S., and Marouf Hasian Jr. "Mourning Absences, Melancholic Commemoration, and the Contested Public Memories of the National September 11 Memorial and Museum." *Western Journal of Communication* 80, no. 2 (2016): 140–162.

Peterson, David. "A New Mission for the Landing." *Star Tribune* (Minneapolis), July 5, 2008.

Pham, Vincent N. "Building and Being a Community Control." *Advances in the History of Rhetoric* 21, no. 3 (2018): 323–325. https://doi.org/10.1080/15362426.2018.1531666.

Phillips, Kendall R. "The Failure of Memory: Reflections on Rhetoric and Public Remembrance." *Western Journal of Communication* 74, no. 2 (2010): 208–223.

Phillips, Lisa. "Wright County Sisters Feted for Their 150-Year-Old Farm." *Delano Eagle* (MN), October 17, 2008.

"Protestors Meet Wagon Train." *MPR News*, May 10, 2008. https://www.mprnews.org/story/2008/05/10/wagonsat.

"Rain on the Scarecrow, Again." *Star Tribune* (Minneapolis), May 16, 2019.

Regan, Paulette. *Unsettling the Settler Within: Indian Residential Schools, Truth Telling, and Reconciliation in Canada*. Chicago: University of Chicago Press, 2011.

Regan, Sheila. "Idle No More Flash Roundy fills Mall of America Rotunda." *TC Daily Planet*, December 30, 2012. https://www.tcdailyplanet.net/idle-no-more-flash-roundy-mall-america.

Richardson, Renee. "Crow Wing Commissioners Split in Vote to Send Resolution Opposing New State Flag." *Brainerd Dispatch*, January 2, 2024.

Riddle, Mason. "Ripple Effects: A Conversation with Angela Two Stars." *Sculpture: A Publication of the International Sculpture Center*, August 11, 2022. https://sculpturemagazine.art/ripple-effects-a-conversation-with-angela-two-stars/.

Rifkin, Mark. *Beyond Settler Time: Temporal Sovereignty and Indigenous Self-Determination.* Durham, Duke University: 2017.

Rifkin, Mark. *When Did Indians Become Straight? Kinship, the History of Sexuality, and Native Sovereignty*. London: Oxford University Press, 2011.

Ross, Jenna. "At Walker, American Indian Artists Discuss the Art World: 'These Changes Need to Be Permanent.'" *Star Tribune* (Minneapolis), March 30, 2018.

Routel, Colette. "Minnesota Bounties on Dakota Men during the U.S.-Dakota War." *William Mitchell Law Review* 40, no. 1 (2013): 1–77.

Schmierbach, Edie. "Cyclist Promotes Land Recovery for Dakota." *Mankato Free Press*

(Mankato, MN), October 13, 2013.

Schudson, Michael. *The Good Citizen: A History of American Civic Life*. Cambridge, MA: Harvard University Press, 1999.

Schultz, Duane P. *Over the Earth I Come: The Great Sioux Uprising of 1862*. New York: St. Martin's Press, 1993.

Selby, Charlene C. "Brownsville to Continue Flying Current Minnesota State Flag." *Filmore County Journal* (Brownsville), January 8, 2024.

Senda-Cook, Samantha, Michael K. Middleton, and Danielle Endres. "Interrogating the 'Field.'" In *Text+Field: Innovations in Rhetorical Method*, edited by Sarah L. McKinnon, Robert Asen, Karma R. Chávez, and Robert Glenn Howard, 22–39. University Park: Pennsylvania State University Press, 2016.

Severson, Gordon. "The Fate of Minnesota's Toppled Christopher Columbus Statue still Undecided More Than a Year Later." *KARE 11*, October 11, 2021. https://www.kare11.com/article/news/local/breaking-the-news/fate-of-minnesotas-toppled-christopher-columbus-statue-still-undecided/89-18f67015-7a99-40b7-bc45-fa7c6aa671d3.

Shakopee Mdewakanton Sioux Community. *2018 Donation Report: Shakopee Mdewakanton Sioux Community.* Prior Lake, MN: Shakopee Mdewakanton Sioux Community, April 15, 2019. https://shakopeedakota.org/resources/smsc-reports-links.

Shakopee Riverfront Cultural Trail: Visitor Experience Plan. Saint Paul: 106 Group, May 28, 2021. https://shakopee.org/wp-content/uploads/2021/07/SRCT-Final-VEP-2021-05-28_reduced.pdf.

Shin, Youjin, Nick Kirkpatrick, Catherine D'Ignazio and Wonyoung So. "Columbus Monuments Are Coming Down, but He's Still Honored in 6,000 Places across the U.S. Here's Where." *Washington Post*, October 26, 2021. https://www.washingtonpost.com/history/interactive/2021/christopher-columbus-monuments-america-map/.

Simpson, Audra. *Mohawk Interruptus: Political Life across the Borders of Settler States*. Durham: Duke University Press, 2014.

———. "The Ruse of Consent and the Anatomy of 'Refusal': Cases from Indigenous North America and Australia." *Postcolonial Studies* 20, no. 1 (2017): 18–33.

———. "Whither Settler Colonialism?" *Settler Colonial Studies* 6, no. 4 (2016): 438–445.

Simpson, Audra, and Andrea Smith, eds. *Theorizing Native Studies*. Durham: Duke University Press, 2016.

Slotkin, Richard. *Gunfighter Nation: The Myth of the Frontier in Twentieth-Century America*. Norman: University of Oklahoma Press, 1998.

Smith, Andrea. "Indigeneity, Settler Colonialism, White Supremacy." In *Racial Formation in the Twenty-First Century*, edited by Daniel Martinez, Ho Sang, and Laursa Pulido, 55–72.

Berkeley: University of California Press, 2012.

———. "Native Studies at the Horizon of Death: Theorizing Ethnographic Entrapment and Settler Self-Reflexivity." In *Theorizing Native Studies*, edited by Audra Simpson and Andrea Smith. Durham: Duke University Press, 2014.

———. "Unsettling the Privilege of Self-Reflexivity." In *Geographies of Privilege*, edited by F. Winndance Twine and B. Gardner. New York: Routledge, 2013.

Smith, Kelly, and Briana Bierschbach. "New Minnesota State Flag Becomes Partisan Issue in 2024." *Star Tribune* (Minneapolis), January 27, 2024. https://www.startribune.com/new-state-flag-becomes-partisan-issue-in-2024/600339023/.

Snelgrove, Corey, Rita Kaur Dhamoon, and Jeff Corntassel. "Unsettling Settler Colonialism: The Discourse and Politics of Settlers, and Solidarity with Indigenous Nations." *Decolonization: Indigeneity, Education & Society* 3, no. 2 (2014): 1–32, https://jps.library.utoronto.ca/index.php/des/article/view/21166.

"Statement to Minnesota House and Finance Committee on House File 274." Minnesota House and Finance Committee. Kevin Jensvold, Tribal Chairperson Upper Sioux Community. February 21, 2023.

St. Paul Pioneer Press. "Dakota Commemorative March Remembers 1862 Forced March to Fort Snelling." November 11, 2012. https://www.twincities.com/2012/11/11/dakota-commemorative-walk-remembers-1862-forced-march-to-fort-snelling/.

Stewart, Ashley. "Minnesota Native Bicycles to Promote Dakota Land." *Blooming Prairie Leader* (MN), October 18, 2013.

Stoesz, John. "Written Support of S.F. 1087." Minnesota State Senate. https://www.senate.mn/committees/2021-2022/3112_Committee_on_Labor_and_Industry_Policy/John%20Stoesz.Written%20sup port%20of%20SF1087.pdf.

"Symbols of the Confederacy Removed Since George Floyd's Death." Southern Poverty Law Center. https://www.splcenter.org/symbols-confederacy-removed-george-floyds-death.

TallBear, Kim. "Annual Meeting: The US-Dakota War and Failed Settler Kinship." *Anthropology News* 57, no. 9 (2016): 92–95.

Taylor, Alan. "The Statues Brought down since the George Floyd Protests Began." *Atlantic*, July 2020.

"The Faribault Cabin." *Landing Journal*, spring 1990, Minnesota Historical Society Gale Family Research Library.

"Their Goal to Live a Traditional, Dakota Lifestyle Will Take an Act of the Legislature." *West Central Tribune* (Granite Falls), February 28, 2020.

The Landing Journal: Murphy's Landing, a Minnesota Valley Restoration of 1840–1890. Gale Family Library, Minnesota Historical Society, spring 1990.

"The Oversized Pop Art of Claes Oldenburg." *CBS Sunday Morning*, aired on December 18, 1994. YouTube. https://www.youtube.com/watch?v=ZrknTntFPdE.

Tuck, Eve, and K. Wayne Yang. "Decolonization Is Not a Metaphor." *Decolonization: Indigeneity, Education & Society* 1, no. 1 (2012): 1–40, https://jps.library.utoronto.ca/index.php/des/article/view/18630.

Tuhiwai Smith, Linda. *Decolonizing Methodologies: Research and Indigenous Peoples*. New York: Zed Books, 2012.

Tully, James. *A Discourse on Property: John Locke and His Adversaries*. New York: Cambridge University Press, 1980.

Turner, Frederick Jackson. "The Significance of the Frontier in American History." American Historical Association, Chicago, July 12, 1893.

"Two Minneapolis Police Officers Were Guilty of Racial Discrimination When They Put Two Drunken Indians in the Trunk of Their Patrol Car for a Trip to the Hospital, a State Agency Ruled Thursday." AP News. https://apnews.com/article/4a387bd09f8cb274ca0cc6d02fefae74.

Two Stars, Angela. "Okciyapi." *Walker Art Museum Magazine*. https://walkerart.org/magazine/okciyapi-angela-two-stars.

"Update on Police Trunk Transport." *MPR* Archive, June 4, 1993. https://archive.mpr.org/stories/1993/06/04/update-on-police-trunk-transport.

Urban Indian Health Institute. *Missing and Murdered Indigenous Women and Girls: A Snapshot of Data from 71 Urban Cities in the United States*. Seattle: Urban Indian Health Institute. http://www.uihi.org/wp-content/uploads/2018/11/Missing-and-Murdered-Indigenous-Women-and-Girls-Report.pdf.

Vail, Mark T. "Reconstructing the Lost Cause in Memphis City Parks Renaming Controversy." *Western Journal of Communication* 76, no. 4 (2012): 417–437.

Veracini, Lorenzo. "Decolonizing Settler Colonialism: Kill the Settler in Him and Save the Man." *American Indian Culture and Research Journal* 41, no. 1 (2017): 1–18.

Viso, Olga. "Learning in Public: An Open Letter on Sam Durant's *Scaffold*." Walker Art Center, May 26, 2017. https://walkerart.org/magazine/learning-in-public-an-open-letter-on-sam-durants-scaffold.

Vivian, Bradford. "The Art of Forgetting: John W. Draper and the Rhetorical Dimensions of History." *Rhetoric & Public Affairs* 2, no. 4 (1999): 551–572.

———. "Jefferson's Other." *Quarterly Journal of Speech* 88, no. 3 (2002): 284–302.

Vogel, Howard J. "The Clash of Stories at Chimney Rock: A Narrative Approach to Cultural Conflict over Native American Sacred Sites on Public Land." *Santa Clara Law Review* 41, no. 3 (2001): 760–761.

———. "Healing the Trauma of America's Past: Restorative Justice, Honest Patriotism, and the Legacy of Ethnic Cleansing." *Buffalo Law Journal* 55, no. 3 (2007): 1006.

———. "Rethinking the Effect of the Abrogation of the Dakota Treaties and the Authority for the Removal of the Dakota People from Their Homeland." *William Mitchell Law Review* 39, no. 2 (2013): 538–581.

Walia, Harsha. "Moving Beyond a Politics of Solidarity Towards a Practice of Decolonization." Colours of Resistance Archive. http://www.coloursofresistance.org/769/moving-beyond-a-politics-of-solidarity-towards-a-practice-of-decolonization/.

"Walker Art Center Announces Artist Angela Two Stars as Finalist for Indigenous Public Art Commission in the Minneapolis Sculpture Garden." Wallker Art Center, September 17, 2019. https://walkerart.org/press-releases/2019/walker-art-center-announces-artist-angela-two-stars-as-finalist-for-indigenous-public-art-commission-in-the-minneapolis-sculpture-garden.

Walsh, Bill. "No One Wants a New Flag." Center for American Experiment, May 10, 2024. https://www.americanexperiment.org/thinking-minnesota-poll-no-one-wants-a-new-flag/.

Wanzer [Wanzer-Serrano], Darrell Allen. "Decolonial Rhetoric and a Future Yet-to-Become: A Loving Response." *Advances in the History of Rhetoric* 21, no. 3 (2018): 326–330, https://doi.org/10.1080/15362426.2018.1526551.

———. "Delinking Rhetoric, or Revisiting McGee's Fragmentation Thesis through Decoloniality." *Rhetoric & Public Affairs* 15, no. 4 (2012): 647–657. https://muse.jhu.edu/article/490122.

Washburn, Terri. "One Hundred and Fifty Years of Farming for Sands Family." *Kenyon Leader* (MN), June 21, 2013.

"Watch Dakota 38 Documentary: Remember Those Lost 150 Years Ago." *Indian Country News*, September 13, 2018. https://ictnews.org/archive/watch-dakota-38-documentary-remember-those-lost-150-years-ago.

Waterman Wittstock, Laura, and Dick Bancroft. *We Are Still Here: A Photographic History of the American Indian Movement*. Saint Paul: Minnesota Historical Society Press, 2013.

Waziyatawin. "The Paradox of Indigenous Resurgence at the End of Empire." *Decolonization: Indigeneity, Education & Society* 1, no. 72 (2012): 68–85. https://jps.library.utoronto.ca/index.php/des/article/view/18629.

———. *What Does Justice Look Like? The Struggle for Liberation in Dakota Homeland*. Saint Paul: Living Justice Press, 2008.

Waziyatawin, Angela Cavender Wilson. "Burning Down the House: Laura Ingalls Wilder and American Colonialism." In *Unlearning the Language of Conquest: Scholars Expose*

Anti-Indianism in America, edited by Four Arrows (Wahinkpe Topa aka Don Trent Jacobs), 66–80. Austin: University of Texas Press, 2006.

———, ed. *In the Footsteps of Our Ancestors: The Dakota Commemorative Marches of the 21st Century*. Saint Paul: Living Justice Press, 2006.

Westerman, Gwen, and Bruce White. *Mni Sota Makoce: The Land of the Dakota*. Saint Paul: Minnesota Historical Society Press, 2012.

White, Bruce. "Tearing Down Fort Snelling—Why It Makes Sense." *Star Tribune* (Minneapolis), April 9, 2009.

"Whose Heritage? Public Symbols of the Confederacy." Southern Poverty Law Center. February 1, 2019. https://www.splcenter.org/20190201/whose-heritage-public-symbols-confederacy.

Williams, Robert A., Jr. *Like a Loaded Weapon: The Rehnquist Court, Indian Rights, and the Legal History of Racism in America*. Minneapolis: University of Minnesota Press, 2005.

Wilson, Angela Cavender. *Unlearning the Language of Conquest*. Edited by Donald Jacobs. Austin: University of Texas Press, 2006.

Wingerd, Mary Lethert. *North Country: The Making of Minnesota*. Minneapolis: University of Minnesota Press, 2010.

Wolfe, Patrick. "Settler Colonialism and the Elimination of the Native." *Journal of Genocide Research* 8, no. 4 (2006): 387–409.

———. "The Settler Complex: An Introduction, Guest Editor." *Settler Colonialism and Native Alternatives in Global Context* 37, no. 2 (2013): 1–22.

Wood, Andrew F. "Haunting Ruins in a Western Ghost Town: Authentic Violence and Recursive Gaze at Bodie, California." *Western Journal of Communication* 84, no. 4 (2020): 439–456.

Woods, Thomas A. *Knights of the Plow: Oliver H. Kelley and the Origins of the Grange in Republican Ideology*. Ames: Iowa State University Press, 1991.

"Works in Progress: Pitted Against the Sky." *New York Times*, April 17, 1988.

Wright, Elizabethada A. "Rhetorical Spaces in Memorial Places: The Cemetery as a Rhetorical Memory Place/Space." *Rhetoric Society Quarterly* 35, no. 4 (2005): 51–80.

Yang, Hannah. "Descendants of Executed Dakota 38+2 Ride to Mankato to Honor Ancestors." *MPR News*, December 23, 2022. https://www.mprnews.org/story/2022/12/23/descendants-of-executed-dakota-382-ride-to-mankato-to-honor-ancestors.

Zelizer, Barbie. "Reading Against the Grain: The Shape of Memory Studies." *Critical Studies in Mass Communication* 12, no. 2 (1995): 214–239.

Index